The
Royal Interiors
of Regency England

The Royal Interiors of Regency England

from watercolours first published by

W. H. Pyne

in 1817–1820

Text by

David Watkin

Peterhouse, Cambridge

Foreword by

Sir Robin Mackworth-Young

Keeper of the Queen's Library

Windsor Castle

J. M. Dent & Sons Ltd

London Melbourne

*The original watercolours commissioned by W.H. Pyne
have been reproduced by gracious permission
of Her Majesty Queen Elizabeth II*

I am greatly indebted to the following who have kindly read the first draft of this book and made numerous valuable corrections and improvements: Sir Oliver Millar, Surveyor of the Queen's Pictures; Mr. Geoffrey de Bellaigue, Surveyor of the Queen's Works of Art; Sir Robin Mackworth-Young, Keeper of the Queen's Library, Windsor Castle; the Hon. Mrs. Hugh Roberts, Curator of the Print Room, Windsor Castle; and Mr. H.M. Colvin, editor of *The History of the King's Works*.

DJW
Peterhouse, Cambridge
1 February 1984

First published in Great Britain 1984
© 1984 The Vendome Press
Reprinted by arrangement with The Vendome Press

Printed and bound in Hong Kong by Mandarin Offset Inc.
for J.M. Dent & Sons Ltd
Aldine House, 33 Welbeck Street, London W1M 8LX

British Library Cataloguing in Publication Data
Watkin, David
   The royal interiors of Regency England from
   watercolours first published by W.H. Pyne,
   1817–20.
   1. Palaces—England—History—19th
   century. 2. Interior architecture—England
   —History—19th century. 3. Architecture,
   Regency.
   I. Title
   725'.17   NA7745
ISBN 0-460-04666-7

Foreword

Large books featuring lavish coloured illustrations of the interiors of celebrated buildings are no rarity today, but at the beginning of the nineteenth century they were unknown. This was not for lack of adequate techniques for coloured reproduction, even at so early a date. The aquatint process, invented in France in the previous century, furnished an excellent foundation in black and white, and there was no shortage of impecunious minor artists to add the colours by hand. Much favoured for the reproduction of their works by English watercolourists, notably by the Windsor artist Paul Sandby, the use of this process for buildings had however been largely confined to exteriors.

In the first decade of the nineteenth century, aquatint was the natural choice for another leading watercolour artist, W.H. Pyne (1769–1843), to adopt in publishing a massive work entitled *Microcosm…of the Arts, Agriculture and Manufactures of Great Britain*. This publication was not concerned with buildings, but contained 'above a thousand groups of small figures for the embellishment of landscape'. Its success encouraged Pyne to undertake further ventures. Subsequent publications involving figures, now with texts by the artist himself, led Pyne into collaboration with Rudolph Ackermann, at that time the leading publisher of prints and illustrated books in London. Ackermann seems however to have valued his associate more as an author than an artist, and actually engaged Pyne to supply the text for several works whose illustrations were contributed by others.

Apparently content to abandon the brush for the pen, Pyne was nevertheless too much of an entrepreneur to surrender the role of publisher indefinitely, and ambition soon led him to a venture of his own as dazzling as it was revolutionary—an illustrated work on the interiors of the royal residences. Exterior views were to be included, but only to set the scene. Since buildings were not his strong point as an artist, it suited Pyne well to follow the pattern established in his relations with Ackermann, and to confine his own contribution to the text, engaging other artists to prepare the watercolours from which the illustrations, 100 in number, were to be made. Well over half (59) were painted by Charles Wild (1781–1835), whose views of English cathedrals were widely reproduced in illustrated books of the period. Of the remainder, 22 were painted by James Stephanoff (c. 1786–1874), history painter and topographer (two illustrations attributed to J. P. Stephanoff and one to L. P. Stephanoff may also be by James), nine by Richard Cattermole (1795–1858), six by William Westall (1781–1850), the most considerable artist of the group, whose contribution was however confined to exterior views, and one (also an exterior) by George Samuel. From these the plates were executed by leading engravers.

In undertaking this work Pyne aimed at a degree of magnificence never before achieved on the printed page. His plans received the early approbation of the Royal Family, without which nothing could have been done. George III having by then lost his reason, permission was obtained to dedicate the first volume to the King's consort, Queen Charlotte (who died before it appeared), and the second and third to the Prince Regent and his brother Frederick Duke of York respectively. Royal approval brought the cooperation from Royal servants that was essential to the success of the project. Not all, however, felt obliged to help. In thanking the Librarian at Frogmore for certain information, Pyne notes drily that he would have been happy to have to acknowledge a similar obligation to the Librarian of Buckingham House. Elsewhere he alludes to 'the forbidding indifference, or the haughtiness of some whose official power enabled them to obstruct his progress'. But these rebuffs appear to have been exceptional, and most royal guardians were generous not only with information but also in the more vital matter of access to the rooms. So was John Nash, the Prince Regent's architect. Nothing, accordingly, seemed to be lacking for the success of the work, and for the financial reward which that success would surely bring.

Four years were to elapse between the first appearance of the advertisement for the work in Ackermann's *Repositories of the Arts* of October 1815 and the publication of the three volumes. In the interval the illustrations were published separately in batches of four as they were completed, without text.

By the time that the volumes appeared there were signs of financial problems. On the last nine plates to be issued the name of Pyne as publisher has been superseded by that of A. Dry, and it is Dry who finally appears as publisher on the title page of each volume, Pyne's role being confined to that of author. A clue to the reason for this change appears in the Advertisement to the first volume, where Pyne reveals that 'an expense of some thousand pounds above the estimate [has] been incurred'.

The notices the work received after its publication in 1819 were nevertheless sufficient to dispel any gloom. 'All that the draughtsman, the engraver, and the print colourer could effect in their respective branches', we read in the *Literary Chronicle and Weekly Review* of 11 March 1820, 'have been devoted to...the very superb embellishments of this truly national work....They are executed with that fidelity which is only to be found in the highest branches of the art. We consider the history of the royal residences to be one of the most magnificent works ever undertaken at the expense of an individual; and we trust that the patronage it will receive will compensate Mr. Pyne for the immense expense at which it has been published; and that those illustrious individuals who must feel a more than common interest in the subject will not be unmindful of the historian of the royal residences'.

The reputation of the work has never flagged from that day to this. It retains its place as a major landmark not only in the history of illustrated books, but also in that of the royal residences themselves, of which many were soon to be drastically reconstructed, and one demolished.

Notwithstanding its reputation, the financial results, by contrast, were disastrous. Illustrious individuals were evidently insufficiently mindful of the author, who was so far ruined by the cost of the illustrations that he was driven to the debtors' prison. 'Fortune did not', we read from his obituary notice in the *Literary Gazette*, 'reward his efforts so liberally as to bless his closing days with the independence he so richly deserved'. It will have been of little comfort to him that he was not the only author/ publisher to sacrifice his solvency on the altar of royal magnificence. A few years after the appearance of *Royal Residences* John Whittaker was to face similar problems in attempting to do justice to the coronation of King George IV.

However magnificent the illustrations, they are nevertheless, and not surprisingly, outshone by the watercolours from which they were derived. Happily a complete set, of identical size to the engravings, has survived in the Royal Library. No evidence has been found about their acquisition, but we may suppose that Pyne would have been forced to sell them when his finances foundered, and that first refusal would have been offered to the owner of the residence, who by that time had ascended the throne as King George IV.

Also preserved in the Royal Library (but not reproduced in the present volume) are larger versions of six of the subjects painted by Wild, each twice the size of its corresponding engraving. These were acquired comparatively recently, five in 1948 and one in 1949. It seems likely that the larger version of each subject was painted first, and the reduced version subsequently copied from it to assist the engraver and the colourist.

A few of the smaller watercolours have been reproduced as isolated illustrations in recent publications. Coloured reproductions have also been made in recent years from the aquatints. A delightful volume by John Cornforth, published by the Folio Society in 1976, included sixteen. The present volume is however the first since those prepared by Pyne to reproduce the watercolours in quantity and in the original. Mindful of Pyne's sad experience, the present publisher has resisted the temptation to include them all; moreover, the diffuse text of the original publication has been replaced by an excellent commentary from the more succinct pen of Dr. David Watkin.

Two other names should be mentioned here. Jane Roberts, the Curator of the Print Room in the Royal Library, whose knowledge has been brought to bear on every section and aspect of this book, including the present introduction, and Nina Lobanov-Rostovski, to whom the original idea was due and without whose enthusiasm this publication might never have been undertaken.

Sir Robin Mackworth-Young

Contents

one

Windsor Castle

Although Windsor Castle is the oldest royal residence to remain in continuous use by the Kings and Queens of England, Pyne's views do not emphasize its romantic antiquity but concentrate almost exclusively on the State Apartments in the Upper Ward as rebuilt in the 1670s for King Charles II. Seldom occupied in the eighteenth century, these apartments would be largely destroyed by Wyatville in the 1820s. Thus, Pyne's record of their appearance could hardly have come at a more miraculously fortunate moment. Only three of the rooms exist today in anything like their seventeenth-century form—the Queen's Presence and Audience Chambers and the King's Dining Room. Meanwhile, St. George's Hall and the adjacent chapel, two of the most important Baroque interiors ever created in England, survive visually only in the watercolours commissioned by Pyne.

Windsor was founded in the late eleventh century by William the Conqueror, who raised the artificial motte on which the Round Tower now stands, and laid out the three baileys or courtyards that survive in plan to this day: the Lower Ward on the west, followed by the Middle Ward in the centre, and the Upper Ward on the east. The castle received its first permanent stone buildings under Henry II in the later twelfth century. The walls of the present Waterloo Chamber and Throne Room date from this period, but it was Edward III in the mid-fourteeth century who built the adjacent royal apartments in the Upper Ward. The bulk of these survives today, although altered by May, Wyatt, and Wyatville. In 1675, their northern section, however, was completely demolished by May, who replaced them with a large, gaunt range, known as the Star Building from its only external adornment, a monumental gilt Garter Star on the north front. But while the architect kept the exterior of this building plain, for the sake of harmony with the massive defensible character of the surrounding medieval walls, he and his associates created interiors in the splendid, up-to-date Baroque manner that Charles II had seen during his exile in Holland and France in the 1650s.

Both Charles II and George IV, who shared many characteristics, fell in love with the historical romance of Windsor, expressing their enthusiasm in extensive building operations. Windsor held immense significance for Charles II as the seat of England's prime order of chivalry, the Order of the Garter, which, founded by Edward III in 1348, came very much to the fore under the Stuarts. Another important association was with the martyred King, Charles I, who lay buried at Windsor. Moreover, at a time when memories of the Civil War were still alive, the castle offered obvious advantages as the only royal residence that was militarily defensible. What Charles II commissioned, and what Pyne shows us room by room, were two sumptuously decorated royal suites: one for himself and one for his Queen, Catharine of Braganza. These apartments, formed partly within the existing Edward III ranges and partly within the new Star Building, were constructed in 1675–78. The second phase, which provided a new royal chapel

OVERLEAF: *Upper Ward, looking towards the Round Tower. This attractive view shows us the quadrangle as remodelled in 1800–13 for George III by James Wyatt, using the castellated style, but before the 1824–40 transformation carried out by his nephew, Wyatville. The tower on the left, known as King Edward III's Tower, had been erected by Henry II in the 1220s. Both the tower and the lower range to its left, built by Edward III in the 1360s, had been remodelled by Hugh May for Charles II in the 1670s with round-headed windows. Wyatt subsequently Gothicized the fenestration of King Edward III's Tower, while Wyatville brought the façade of the lower range forward so as to provide space for a continuous access corridor round the royal apartments in the Upper Ward. The range on the extreme right in Wild's watercolour, with the Royal Chapel and St. George's Hall at first-floor level, is also the work of Edward III, although, again, it had been classicized by May and re-Gothicized by Wyatt. Wyatville left this untouched save for the entrance tower, which he rebuilt to make it project much farther into the courtyard. Wyatville was also to increase the height of the Round Tower by over 30 feet by adding its great stone collar. In the foreground of Wild's view stands the bronze equestrian statue of Charles II, cast in 1679 and mounted on a high stone base with decorative carvings by Grinling Gibbons. During Wyatville's reconstruction the statue was moved from the centre of the quadrangle to its present position immediately below the Round Tower.* View by C. Wild.

and St. George's Hall, got under way in 1678, with the structural work completed by 1680 and the interior decoration four years later. Designed in an Anglo-Dutch version of the French Baroque style then being adopted for Louis XIV, the new interiors at Windsor were the result of a collaboration between the architect Hugh May, who had spent the years of the Commonwealth in Holland; the Italian decorator Antonio Verrio, who, during his stay in Paris in 1671, had been influenced by the work of Charles Le Brun; the brilliant carver Grinling Gibbons, born in Rotterdam of English parents; and the French gilder René Cousin. What the builder and his artists produced were the first interiors in England that echoed the unified treatment characteristic of the Italian Baroque, the walls painted with figures seen through simulated screens of columns, and the ceilings with sky effects containing gods and goddesses. Verrio subsequently decorated in a similar vein interiors at great houses such as Burghley, Cassiobury, Chatsworth, Ham, and Moor Park.

The duplication of royal apartments for the King and Queen had become a feature of English palaces by the late Middle Ages.

Ballroom. This detail from the plate on pages 22–23 shows Grinling Gibbons's richly carved cornice and the elaborate silver chandelier that survived from the late-seventeenth-century taste for luxury.

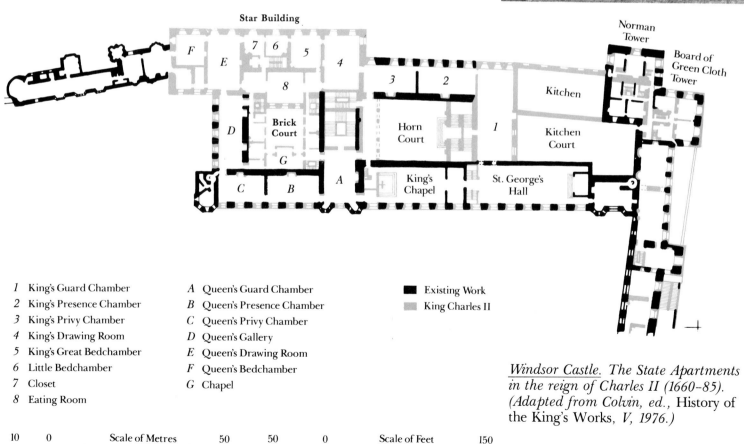

1 King's Guard Chamber
2 King's Presence Chamber
3 King's Privy Chamber
4 King's Drawing Room
5 King's Great Bedchamber
6 Little Bedchamber
7 Closet
8 Eating Room

A Queen's Guard Chamber
B Queen's Presence Chamber
C Queen's Privy Chamber
D Queen's Gallery
E Queen's Drawing Room
F Queen's Bedchamber
G Chapel

■ Existing Work
▨ King Charles II

Windsor Castle. The State Apartments in the reign of Charles II (1660–85). (Adapted from Colvin, ed., History of the King's Works, *V, 1976.)*

10   0   Scale of Metres   50   50   0   Scale of Feet   150

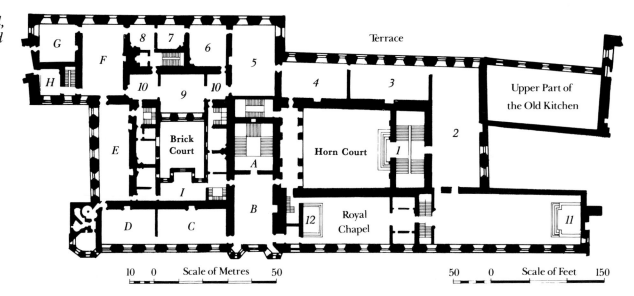

Windsor Castle. Upper Ward, north side, in 1790. (Adapted from Downes, English Baroque Architecture, *1966.)*

1   King's Stair
2   King's Guard Chamber
3   King's Presence Chamber
4   King's Audience Chamber
5   King's Withdrawing Room
6   King's Bedchamber
7   King's Dressing Room
8   King's Closet
9   King's Dining Room
10 Lobby
11 Throne
12 Altar

A   Queen's Stair
B   Queen's Guard Chamber
C   Queen's Presence Chamber
D   Queen's Audience Chamber
E   Queen's Ballroom
F   Queen's Drawing Room
G   Queen's Bedchamber
H   Ante-room
I   Private Chapel

The maintenance of that tradition by Charles II is obvious. Less clear, however, even in Pyne's day and certainly in ours, is the purpose of the individual rooms. It may be helpful to consider the sequence of State Rooms as a kind of frozen memorial of the gradual retreat of the sovereign from the public, or rather of the endless encroachment on his privacy by his ministers, courtiers, and subjects. The essential rooms in the early medieval palace had been the Great Hall and the Chamber, the latter subject to use by the King for both sleeping and holding councils. Tudor palaces contained three essential rooms: the Guard Chamber, the Presence Chamber, in which the monarch gave audiences, and the Privy Chamber. Beyond the Privy Chamber there would be a bedroom. By the time of Charles II those seeking audience had invaded the Privy Chamber, so that a 'withdrawing' room was inserted between it and the bedroom. The withdrawing room, in turn, had become a public room by the early eighteenth century. All this would indicate that the rooms did not supersede one another but, as a modern authority has put it, each 'merely added one more unit to the suite'. Furthermore, 'each room retained its appropriate attendants—the Yeomen of the Guard in the Guard Chamber, the Gentlemen Ushers in the Presence Chamber, the Gentlemen of the Privy Chamber in the Privy Chamber, and the Groom of the Stole in the Drawing Room and the private rooms beyond. Each of the principal reception rooms might still boast its canopy of state, marking the position where the King had once sat, one, two, or three hundred years before. The history of the court was therefore encapsulated in the State Apartments of the English royal palaces as they existed in the reign of George III'.[1]

Charles II, who died in 1685, did not have long to enjoy the golden glow of the triumphalism that May, Verrio, and Gibbons had created for him in his rooms of parade. Following the Revolution of 1688, and the acceptance of the crown by William III in the following year, Windsor entered into a long sleep. Queen Anne was the only monarch in the eighteenth century who inhabited the State Apartments, although the Hanoverian

sovereigns occasionally used them for ceremonial occasions. After the death of Queen Anne in 1714, parts of the castle became unofficial grace-and-favour residences, and when George I visited Windsor he stayed in the Garden House. This was a modest dwelling outside the castle walls that, owing to its association with Queen Anne, would come to be known as Queen's Lodge. It was enlarged in 1776–79 by George III, who also employed Sir William Chambers in 1779–82 to rebuild on a larger scale another house on the edge of the town, Lower Lodge, in order to accommodate his growing family. Remodelled in 1842, Lower Lodge survives today as Burford House.

In the meantime, George III's interest in the castle itself was growing. In 1782 the King began his 'improvements' to the great medieval chapel of St. George's, Windsor, and in 1789, once recovered from his illness, he decided to take up residence in the castle. This was a romantic and surprising decision, rather as though the present Queen and the Duke of Edinburgh were to move back to Hampton Court. The King employed James Wyatt to make various revisions in the State Apartments during the 1790s, but the main campaign began in 1800, and by 1804 it had advanced sufficiently to enable the sovereign to take up residence, the first to do so since Queen Anne. Work on Wyatt's alterations continued at enormous expense but remained incomplete in 1811, when George III entered the final nine-year period of his illness. It was towards the end of this melancholy time that Pyne's artists began their task of recording the desolate State Apartments. Within half a dozen years Wyatville's men would be busy destroying most of May's interiors and replacing them with a palatial suite in an eclectic array of styles from Gothic to Rococo. Between 1824 and 1840 a million pounds was spent in remodelling, extending, and restoring the castle, providing it with a new range of magnificent State Apartments in the east range of the Upper Ward, and creating the incomparably romantic skyline that has stirred the souls of visitors ever since as a quintessentially Picturesque expression of British national identity.

Staircase. What Pyne describes as this 'magnificent Gothic staircase' was inserted by James Wyatt in 1800–04 on the site of the Queen's Grand Staircase and the adjacent Privy Staircase erected by May in the 1670s. Richly decorated by Verrio, May's staircase was a domed Baroque extravaganza, while Wyatt's was dominated by a high octagonal lantern, nearly 100 feet above floor level, and ornamented with Gothic plasterwork by Bernasconi. This staircase was in turn removed by Wyatville, who provided a grand new flight immediately to the west in Brick Court. However, the Bernasconi ceiling survives intact in the Grand Vestibule, although its crowning octagon was remodelled in 1834. In 1866, after the approach to Wyatville's staircase proved too dark, Salvin replaced the whole arrangement with the present Grand Staircase. View by C. Wild.

Old Guard Chamber in the Round Tower. This interior was drastically altered by Wyatville in 1830–31 when he remodelled the twelfth-century Round Tower, doubling it in height by adding a kind of stone collar on top of the original exterior walls. This view shows the Old Guard Chamber with armour laid out decoratively by Charles II's cousin, Prince Rupert, who was appointed Constable of the Castle in 1668. The panelling and woodwork may date from a refitting carried out under Queen Anne in 1702–06. The history of the display of contemporary arms in the royal guard chambers at Windsor Castle, St. James's Palace, and Hampton Court in the seventeenth century is somewhat obscure. It seems to have been a particularly English development, which was related to a taste then current in North European courts but less readily parallelled in Italy, France, and Spain. View by J. Stephanoff.

Kitchen. The great kitchen of the medieval castle, bustling with activity in
this view, is a two-storeyed apartment built in the fourteenth century against
the north outer wall of the Upper Ward. Shortly after Stephanoff painted the
room it was remodelled by Wyatville with a new lantern and windows. It
continues in use as a kitchen today. View by J. Stephanoff.

Queen's Drawing Room. The room is dominated by the six charming landscapes painted in the 1740s by Francesco Zuccarelli (1702–88), who, after his arrival in 1752, spent nearly twenty years in England and became a founder-member of the Royal Academy in 1768. The practice of hanging pictures on top of tapestry may appear odd to us, but it can be seen in numerous interiors recorded in Pyne's Royal Residences and survives to this day in the Long Gallery at Hardwick Hall.

Verrio's ceiling, destroyed by Wyatville, was purely mythological in subject: the Assembly of the Gods. The view painted by Wild reveals the floor to have been left uncarpeted, as in the other rooms of the Queen's Apartment. View by C. Wild.

ABOVE: *Queen's Guard Chamber. This was the first room the visitor entered in the sequence of the Queen's State Rooms laid out by May in the 1670s on the south and west sides of Brick Court. Verrio's triumphal ceiling depicts Queen Catharine of Braganza with the Four Continents paying her homage. The Queen's Guard Chamber, which led to the adjacent Queen's Grand Staircase, was remodelled by Wyatville when he formed the present entrance lobby. Wild shows the room fitted out temporarily as a chapel by George III in 1804, at a time when the King had begun to dismantle May's chapel with a view to Gothicizing it. View by C. Wild.*

ABOVE: *Queen's Presence Chamber.* Carved by Grinling Gibbons and Henry Phillips, the sumptuous festoons of fruit and flowers and the cornice date from 1677–78. The ceiling painting, one of the three that survive of the twenty executed by Verrio in the State Apartments at Windsor, shows the Queen attended by the Virtues, with Justice driving out the forces of evil. The portraits on the left wall, all by van Dyck, are of Charles I, James I, over the chimney, and Charles I with Henrietta Maria and their children, Charles, Prince of Wales, and Mary, Princess Royal. At the far end hangs a portrait of an unknown knight of the Golden Fleece, painted in the studio of Rubens. The chimney-piece in the room today was brought by William IV from the Saloon at Buckingham House (p. 82). View by C. Wild.

OPPOSITE: *Queen's State Bedchamber.* In 1804 James Wyatt had nearly doubled the size of this room, by incorporating the staircase and closet on the south side. The view shows the original State Bedchamber with its Verrio ceiling of Diana and

Endymion, which John Rigaud had matched in 1805 over the new area, where the subject became Jupiter presenting Diana with her bow and arrows. The new walls were then painted red. Stephanoff's watercolour, showing the unusual Baroque-revival ceiling, is the only visual record we have of a room that was completely refurbished in the reign of William IV as part of the suite housing the Royal Library. The Louis XV commode of japanned pearwood with gilt-bronze mounts survives in the Royal Collection. The paintings seen by Stephanoff included ten portraits by Lely traditionally known as 'The Windsor Beauties'; however, they now hang at Hampton Court. View by J. Stephanoff.

Ballroom. This was actually the Queen's Gallery,
which had a Verrio ceiling peopled with figures of
Perseus and Andromeda symbolizing the liberation of
Europe by Charles II. The room was subsequently
dismantled by Wyatville, all but Gibbons's cornice,
which remains intact. Wild shows the room as altered
by Wyatt, who modified the windows and removed the
Brussels tapestries that formerly hung on the walls.
The citizens of London had presented Charles II and
William III with silver furniture, some of which
appears in the present view. The silver tables,
chandeliers, and andirons are superb examples of a
late-seventeenth-century taste for luxury, which can
also be seen in some of the furniture at Knole. View
by C. Wild.

King's Closet. Sometimes known as the Queen's Closet, this room, as left by May, was quite small, and Wyatt had enlarged it in 1804, replacing Verrio's ceiling of Leda and the Swan with a painting by Wyatt's youngest son, Matthew Cotes Wyatt. It represents St. George and the Dragon, a subject more in keeping with George III's romantic nationalism. But Wild's view is the sole record we have of M.C. Wyatt's ceiling, since Wyatville, on commission from William IV, eliminated it in favour of ornamental plasterwork. Wild shows the walls hung with scarlet cloth, which forms a background for the collection of royal portraits and Old Master paintings. The writing table on the right, decorated with seaweed marquetry, was made in c. 1690 by Gerreit Jensen for William III. View by C. Wild.

King's Dressing Room. *Adjacent to the King's Closet was another small room that originally had a Verrio ceiling, in this case depicting Jupiter and Danae. By the time Wild painted his view M.C. Wyatt had replaced the Verrio work with scenes from the life of Saint George. In the reign of Charles II the room had served as the King's little bedchamber. The wall hangings and pictures seen here echo those in the King's Closet. Simple rush matting covers the floor. View by C. Wild.*

BELOW: *King's State Bedchamber. Verrio's ceiling depicted Charles II in the robes of the Garter with the Four Continents paying homage to him. Wyatville left the cornice intact but replaced the ceiling with a plaster composition incorporating the arms of the Stuarts. The Gothic traceried windows at the north end had been inserted by Wyatt for George III. This room was the last in the sequence of three the walls of which were hung with scarlet cloth. View by C. Wild.*

OPPOSITE: *King's Drawing Room. This shows one of Verrio's most ambitious ceilings,* a depiction of the restoration of the monarchy in 1660, symbolized by Charles II driving through the sky in a triumphal car. The painting was destroyed by Wyatville, who added an oriel window at the north end looking out towards Eton. At the south end we can see through the open door to Wyatt's Gothic staircase. The walls were a soft mauve colour, forming a background to Baroque paintings, among them the Toilet of Venus, *from the studio of Guido Reni, and a copy of this artist's* Perseus and Andromeda. *Bought by George I in 1723, these were given by William IV to the National Gallery. View by J. Stephanoff.*

OPPOSITE: <u>King's Eating Room</u>. Pyne's caption, 'Queen Anne's Bed', refers to the state bed that George III piously preserved in the former dining room of Charles II. According to Pyne, 'he would not displace the venerable relic for the most splendid bed in the universe'. It can now be seen at Hampton Court. In this room George II ate in public on stated days, in the manner of Louis XIV at Versailles. Above the English King floated Verrio's ceiling composition devoted to the Banquet of the Gods. This survives, as do the coves painted enticingly with fish and fowl. Wild shows the walls to have been hung with scarlet cloth in place of Gibbons's and Phillips's exquisite woodcarvings of fruit, fish, game, and shellfish, which had recently been removed to Hampton Court. Today they once again adorn the King's Eating Room at Windsor. In the nineteenth century the alcoves for musicians and servants at the west and east ends were provided with skylights and thrown into the main body of the

dining room, from which they are approached through segmental arched openings. These help give the room a certain early Victorian flavour despite the seventeenth-century fittings. View by C. Wild.

ABOVE: <u>King's Audience Chamber</u>. This is one of the most interesting watercolours since it shows an interior by May as altered for George III in the 1780s but before its complete remodelling and reduction in size by Wyatville in the 1820s to serve as the Ante-Throne Room. George III retained Verrio's ceiling, which depicted the re-establishment of the Church of England in 1660, but added the neo-classical chimney-piece, gilded the cornice and mouldings, and fitted the walls with Garter-blue, flower-bordered silk as a background to a series of eight paintings specially commissioned from Benjamin West in

1787–89. Seven of these, which marked an important stage in the development of eighteenth-century history painting, represented the exploits of the Black Prince and Edward III, including the institution by the latter of the Order of the Garter. The painting seen in Wild's view to the right of the chimney-piece shows Edward and the Black Prince after the Battle of Crécy in 1346. It is now on loan at the Palace of Westminster. Over the chimney-piece hangs West's painting, now at Hampton Court, of St. George slaying the Dragon. Other additions made by George III include the striking new chair of state and canopy, hung with dark-blue valances adorned with garlands of flowers executed, from designs by Mary Moser, at Mrs. Pawsey's school of needlework at Ampthill. It was supported at the back by Biagio Rebecca's arabesque-painted pilasters and adorned with West's medallions portraying George III and his Queen. View by C. Wild.

———

Royal Chapel. This splendid room, probably the finest Baroque interior ever assembled in England, was destroyed by Wyatville and incorporated into May's adjacent St. George's Hall so as to form the present St. George's Hall, a room in a mechanical Gothic style, 180 feet long and only 30 feet wide, which occupies most of the southern range of the State Apartments. The walls of May's chapel, as recorded by Pyne, were painted in trompe l'oeil with twisted Baroque columns that framed at the west (liturgical east) end Verrio's altar piece of the Last Supper beneath a simulated semi-dome. The illusionistic ceiling depicted the Resurrection with clouds and angels flowing over the trompe l'oeil coffering, while the north wall was painted with Christ healing the sick, among them, by a happy touch, figures of Verrio and May. The chapel, which already looked like a place of Roman Catholic worship, actually served that purpose in the reign of James II. In Pyne's day, however, the altar painting had been removed and the chapel partly dismantled. Of the view rendered by Wild, all that survives in the castle today are some of Gibbons's carved lime-wood sprays of palm and laurel from the niches behind the choir stalls, reused in the Waterloo Chamber. Meanwhile, the church of St. John Baptist, built in Windsor High Street in 1820–22, contains part of Gibbons's balustered communion rail with panels of foliage and pelicans in their piety. View by C. Wild.

BELOW: _King's Guard Chamber._ The first room in Charles II's State Apartment, this somber interior was hung with military trophies and lit by a glazed octagonal lantern decorated by Verrio with a painting of Jupiter and Juno enthroned. A topographer in 1749 recorded that the trophies round the walls were 'ranged by Mr. Harris, late Master-Gunner of this Castle, the same person who made that beautiful Arrangement of the small Arms in the Great Armory in the Tower of London'.[2] Here Verrio used watercolour, not oil as elsewhere at Windsor, and the paintings had thus deteriorated considerably when Wyatville transformed the King's Guard Room into the present Grand Reception Room. The splendour of this glittering neo-Rococo interior more than compensates for the loss of the Verrio paintings shown by Wild. View by C. Wild.

OPPOSITE: _St. George's Hall._ There can be no doubt that the destruction in the 1820s of this room and of the chapel into which it led was one of the major tragedies in the history of English architecture. Pyne can have had no conception that within less than a decade the hall which he described as 'one of the most spacious and magnificent in Europe' would be no more. Verrio's Baroque paintings

flowed round the room with, on the left in Wild's view, scenes of the Black Prince
received in triumph by Edward III, while in the central oval of the ceiling,
Charles II in Garter robes sat enthroned in glory. Trompe l'oeil Corinthian
columns divided the walls into bays. The carving was by Grinling Gibbons and the
extensive gilding by the ubiquitous René Cousin, whose work helped unite the room
decoratively. At the end of the hall we can see the French tricolor, which even
today is presented annually to the sovereign by the Duke of Wellington as 'rent' for
Stratfield Saye House. View by C. Wild.

on the right in Wild's view we can see the wooden oriel that Henry VIII added in the 1520s to the chantry chapel of Edward IV (d. 1483), founder of the present St. George's Chapel. Built for Queen Catharine of Aragon, the oriel unites in its decoration both Gothic and Renaissance features. The iron screen beneath it was made by John Tresilian in c. 1480 and remains one of the finest pieces of its kind in the country. View by C. Wild.

OPPOSITE: *Royal Chapel of St. George's, Windsor, looking east.* Built in 1475–1528, St. George's Chapel is one of the three royal masterpieces in the Perpendicular style, the others being King's College Chapel, Cambridge, and Henry VII's Chapel, Westminster Abbey. Wild's view holds particular interest as a record of the appearance of the choir after its refurbishment in 1785–91 for George III by the architect Henry Emlyn and the painter Benjamin West. Emlyn removed the tracery of the east window to accommodate a painted glass, or 'transparency', depicting the Resurrection, a work executed by West, as was the large altar painting of the Last Supper. In 1863, however, during a campaign planned as a memorial to Prince Albert, tracery was reinserted in the east window, which Clayton and Bell then filled with glass. West's altar-piece was hung in a less prominent position elsewhere in the chapel and replaced with an alabaster reredos by J.B. Philip. Meanwhile, Emlyn's convincingly Perpendicular Coade stone organ-screen survives today. View by C. Wild.

Royal Chapel of St. George's, Windsor, looking west.
St. George's is the chapel of the Order of the Garter, not the domestic chapel of the castle. To serve the ceremonial needs of the Order the choir was planned with three tiers of stalls: the upper for the Knights of the Garter, the Dean and Canons; the middle for the Military Knights, Minor Canons, and choirmen; and the lowest for the choirboys. The heraldic banners of the Knights hang above their elaborately canopied stalls, set up in 1478–85, the backs of which bear their enamelled heraldic plates. The sovereign's stall stands on the left of the central entrance door from the nave. The organ case is an early monument of the Gothic Revival, erected in 1790 for George III from designs by Henry Emlyn. In the first bay

two
Hampton
Court

*I*n Pyne's day, Hampton Court had about it the same lingering air of romance as the modern visitor finds even now. The story of the sensational downfall of Cardinal Wolsey, the intimate associations with Henry VIII and five of his unhappy wives, the survival intact of Wren's State Apartments for William and Mary, unused since the reign of George II, the Thames-side gardens and park with their maze, vine, and avenues—all this has become deeply embedded in the Englishman's sense of historical identity. And it probably lodges there side by side with childhood memories of his own first visit, for the State Apartments have been open free to the public since the early days of Victoria's reign.

In the 1530s, after Henry VIII acquired the great Tudor palace begun in 1514 by Wolsey, Hampton Court was extended until it became one of the largest houses in sixteenth-century Europe. The Perpendicular Gothic style of the previous century governs the rambling courtyards of warm red brick, with their towers, turrets, and oriels, making the palace less a reflection of the Italian Renaissance than was François I's exactly contemporary château of Chambord, which both Wolsey and Henry undoubtedly hoped to rival. Indeed, Renaissance motifs are confined to the celebrated terracotta roundels of Roman Emperors on the gatehouses, executed by Giovanni da Maiano in 1512, to gilded plaster ceilings such as that in Wolsey's cabinet, and to the decorated spandrels and pendants of the hall and chapel ceilings.

Henry VIII's royal apartments were destroyed by Wren, who fortunately spared the Chapel Royal, the Great Kitchen, and the grandest of the Tudor King's additions to the palace, the Great Hall. However, Henry VIII had helped establish the sequence of rooms in a State Apartment so as to regulate the access that courtiers and others had to the monarch. Where once the Hall and the King's Chamber had been sufficient, now there evolved a succession of rooms, beginning with the Guard Chamber, which housed the Yeomen of the Guard founded by Henry VII, then continued with the Presence Chamber, in which the King granted audiences, followed by the Privy Chamber, the sovereign's private retiring room, to which visitors rarely penetrated, and finally the Bedchamber. We have already noted at Windsor how in the seventeenth century, the attempt to keep the Privy Chamber private having failed, a withdrawing room was inserted before the Bedchamber. In due course this too would become a public reception room. Even before the age of the newspaper reporter and the television cameraman, the English public pursued their royal family relentlessly.

Because of the loss of the original State Apartments, most of the Hampton Court interiors recorded by Pyne are the ones that Sir Christopher Wren created for William and Mary. The asthmatic William III never cared for the foggy, damp, low-lying palace of Whitehall, and even before the disastrous fires that destroyed most of it in 1691 and 1698, he had commissioned Wren to turn Hampton Court into something more like Louis XIV's Versailles. Initially, according to plans prepared in 1689, Wren envisaged the

OVERLEAF: *Hampton Court, park front. The east or park front of the palace was designed and built by Sir Christopher Wren for William III in 1689–95 as a deliberately discreet echo of the splendours of Versailles. It became Wren's final statement of finely jointed, warm, red brickwork combined with Portland stone dressings. The King wanted the rooms on the* piano nobile *to be raised as little as possible above ground level, perhaps because his asthma made it difficult for him to climb stairs. Thus, Wren's pedimented centrepiece on the east front rests on a low and unimpressive plinth, and indeed the first, or main, floor window-sills are not supported by solid stonework but float above the voids of the ground-floor trabeated doorways. The pedimental sculpture, representing the Triumph of Hercules over Envy and dating from 1694, was carved by Caius Gabriel Cibber in symbolical allusion to William III's victories in the war against France.* View by W. Westall.

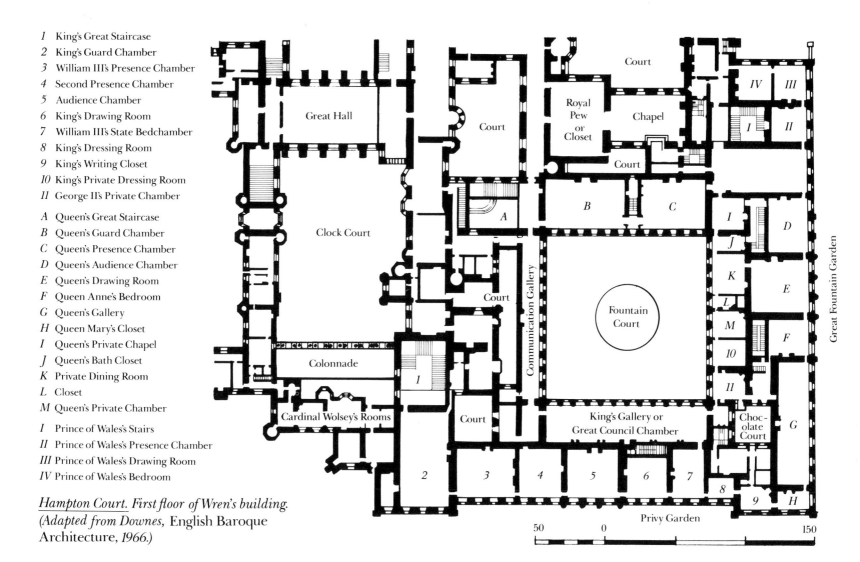

Hampton Court. First floor of Wren's building. (Adapted from Downes, English Baroque Architecture, *1966.)*

destruction of the whole Tudor palace, save for the Great Hall, which was to have been isolated as the climax of a grand approach from the north. The royal apartments were to be rebuilt on their old site south-east of the hall round a vast rectangular court aligned on Charles II's Long Canal. With its echoes of Versailles and of Bernini's unexecuted project for the Louvre, all this would have produced one of the great palaces of Europe. However, the passing of the Bill of Rights later in 1689 put an end to the Divine Right of Kings and transferred power to Parliament. Government, now established at Westminster, would no longer follow the King from palace to palace. Thus; certain features of Wren's palace, such as the proposed suite of rooms centred on the Council Chamber, as well as the whole absolutist scale, came to seem inappropriate. The outcome of this was that half of the Tudor palace remained intact, while the new royal apartments provided by Wren in 1689–94 were grouped round a much smaller court than the one the architect had originally projected. This new court, Fountain Court, retained the Tudor disposition of rooms, with the King's suite or apartment in the south range overlooking the privy garden, and the Queen's in the east range facing across the park. The abrupt juxtaposition of Wren's palatial classicism with the lower ranges in the Tudor

Gothic style, which would be most unusual in a royal palace on the Continent, scarcely shocks English eyes, accustomed as they are to similar contrasts in the colleges of Oxford and Cambridge.

Work on Wren's new ranges proceeded rapidly. Although the interiors had yet to be decorated, the building was largely complete by December 1694 when the Queen died of smallpox. The heartbroken William stopped the work but resumed it after the second fire at Whitehall four years later. Wren now began the decoration and furnishing of the King's Apartment, leaving the decoration of the Queen's Apartment to be continued under Queen Anne after William's death in 1702 and finally completed for the Prince and Princess of Wales in 1715–18. Wren's magnificent but carefully understated architecture, studded with fine carving by Cibber and Gibbons, ironwork by Tijou, and decorative painting by Thornhill, Verrio, Laguerre, and Kent, has always been recognized as one of the high points of English artistic achievement. Having recently defeated Louis XIV in arms and checked his ambitions for dominating Europe, William and his advisors made sure that the decoration of the new Hampton Court would everywhere refer to military triumph. The views prepared for Pyne are a handsome tribute to the imaginative genius of Wren and of his superb team of decorators. The only regret is that the watercolours are so comparatively few in number.

OPPOSITE: *Grand Stair. Wren's Grand Staircase to the King's Apartment was formed in 1690–91 within the pre-existing Tudor structures at the south-east angle of the Clock Court. It is approached externally by the dramatic open colonnade of coupled Ionic columns with which Wren concealed the south side of the Tudor court. The staircase, which runs round three sides of a large and airy rectangular well, is adorned with Tijou's beautiful wrought-iron balustrade and with Verrio's illusionistic Baroque paintings, their figures crowding dramatically in front of the trompe l'oeil colonnade. The theme of the paintings, which date from c. 1700, is a curious one, based on Julian the Apostate's satire,* The Caesars, *where Alexander the Great is regarded as preferable to all the Caesars. One interpretation of the somewhat problematical iconography sees Alexander as the Protestant William III and the Roman Emperors as the objectionable Roman Catholics!* View by G. Cattermole

Cartoon Gallery. A detail from the plate on page 47, with one of the great Raphael tapestry cartoons displayed on the end wall.

OPPOSITE: _Chapel_. Although completed under Henry VIII in 1535–56 and subsequently refitted and redecorated under Queen Anne, the Chapel Royal at Hampton Court belongs in its bones to Wolsey's palace. Henry's magnificent timber roof, with its great pendants and stars of lierne vaulting, offers a striking example of late Perpendicular craftsmanship, comparable with the stone vault of Henry VII's chapel at Westminster Abbey. In 1710–11 Queen Anne spent over £4,000 on panelling and carving, including the great Baroque reredos, all executed by Hopson and Gibbons, and on decorative paintings by Thornhill. The fittings were added as a conscious statement of the Queen's commitment to High Church Anglicanism. View by C. Wild.

ABOVE: _Guard Chamber_. Approached from the staircase, this is the first room in the King's Apartment decorated under the direction of Wren and Talman in 1699. The 3,000 pieces of

armour that adorn it were arranged in patterns under Wren's supervision for William III. View by J. Stephanoff.

OVERLEAF: _First Presence Chamber_. Pyne describes the aquatint made from this watercolour as a view of the Throne Room at Hampton Court, but in his day the room had been left unused for almost sixty years, so that its original function could no longer be known for certain. Actually, it was the second chamber in the State Apartment and contained, as it still does today, a canopy and a chair of state covered in crimson damask. In Stephanoff's painting the case cover over the chair gives it an almost suburban look. The walls are hung with superb sixteenth-century Brussels tapestries, later removed to Windsor, depicting the Triumph of Bacchus and the Labours of Hercules. In Pyne's day the hangings were largely obscured by pictures, which included, on either side of the chimney-piece, a Tintoretto and a Bonifazio, the latter formerly attributed to Palma Vecchio. View by J. Stephanoff.

BELOW: *Second Presence Chamber. In Stephanoff's view of this room, which contains no chair of state, the east wall is panelled while the north wall is hung with tapestry as a background for paintings, among them a copy of van Dyck's great equestrian portrait of Charles I at Windsor. Over the doors hang interesting ruin pieces by Jacques Rousseau (1630–93) that anticipated the capriccio paintings of Panini in the next* century. They have been there and in the Eating Room continuously from the time of Queen Anne to the present day. Pyne describes the remainder of the King's Apartment—the Audience Chamber with its canopy, the Drawing Room, the Bedchamber with its Verrio ceiling and crimson velvet bed with gold lace and ostrich plumes, the Dressing Room, and the small Writing Closet—but, sadly, illustrates only the last of these. The

Queen's Apartment similarly contained a network of smaller rooms where Her Majesty could escape from the grandeur and the chill of the public rooms. View by J. Stephanoff.

=======

OVERLEAF: Queen Mary's State Bedchamber. This dashing evocation of a Baroque room of state, although described by Pyne as the bedroom of Queen Mary, did not receive the form in which Cattermole shows it until after the monarch's death, when it was panelled and decorated for George, Prince of Wales (later George II), in 1714–15. At that time the ceiling was painted by Thornhill with a scene of Leucothoë, daughter of the King of Babylon, restraining Apollo from entering his chariot. Pyne, like many others, misinterpreted this somewhat arcane

subject as 'Aurora rising from the ocean in a chariot drawn by white horses'. On the cove appear figures of slaves and cupids supporting medallions of George I and the Prince of Wales, Caroline, Princess of Wales, and their son, Prince Frederick. The crimson damask state bed, which still survives, was apparently preserved by George III as a relic of Queen Mary. However, it was not made for her but later, in 1715, for the Prince of Wales. The outer hangings are not properly part of the bed, but simply case curtains added in order to protect the damask draperies beneath. View by G. Cattermole.

=======

ABOVE: Queen's Gallery. Pyne describes this as the 'Ball-Room...also called the Tapestry Gallery', although it originated

as the Long Gallery of the Queen's Apartment. The Le Brun tapestries of Alexander the Great were acquired by George I, while the striking marble chimney-piece was carved in 1700 by John Nost for the King's Bedchamber, only to be transferred almost immediately to the Queen's Gallery. It is a lively piece embellished with a scrolled pediment, two cupids, two doves, and a bust of Venus. Almost equally exuberant are the forms of the ornate tables, candelabra, and stools that line the walls. View by G. Cattermole.

———————————

<u>Cartoon Gallery.</u> The seven superlative Raphael cartoons of 1515–16, acquired by Charles I and described by Pyne as 'almost divine', were hung in the Long Gallery of the King's Apartment, overlooking Fountain Court, in November 1698. By the end of the following year the decoration of the room had been completed, with carvings by Grinling Gibbons, including the twenty-five Corinthian capitals, for which the sculptor received £572. John Nost carved the handsome chimney-piece of purple, black, and white marble with gilt-brass ornaments and a carved frieze representing the Triumph of Venus. The cartoons were removed to the Saloon at Buckingham House in 1763 and to the State Apartments at Windsor in 1787, but then returned to Hampton Court in 1809 at the instance of the Prince of Wales. Since 1865 they have been on permanent loan to the Victoria and Albert Museum, their place in the Cartoon Gallery at Hampton Court having been taken by a set of early-seventeenth-century tapestries woven from them. View by J. Stephanoff.

three

St. James's Palace

Built round four courtyards by Henry VIII in the 1530s, St. James's Palace is, in both form and function, one of the more picturesque curiosities associated with the British Crown. It occupies the site of a hospital for leper maidens that had been dissolved in 1532, and stands as an engaging witness to the Tudor King's mania for building palaces. Still today Ambassadors are formally accredited to the Court of St. James, although no monarch has resided in the palace for over two centuries. The numerous additions made after the Restoration in 1660 culminated in the full suite of State Rooms built by Sir Christopher Wren for Queen Anne in 1703 on the south side of Engine Court and the west side of Paradise Court. Most of these survive today, although somewhat altered and occasionally known by different names. Levees, drawing rooms, and audiences took place in them throughout the eighteenth century. Arriving in the Guard Room, visitors passed through the Presence Chamber (today Tapestry Room) at the centre of the long south front. From here they might turn left, i.e., to the east, and pass through the Little Drawing Room (which Pyne called the Queen's Levee Room) and into the King's Bedchamber next door, where the sovereign sometimes granted audiences to his ministers. Or they might turn right into the Drawing Room (today the Entree Room) and adjacent Council Chamber (now the Throne Room). Here drawing rooms and levees were held. Levees, attended only by men, took place on Wednesday and Friday mornings and might last as long as three hours. Until the first of George III's illnesses in 1788, they were also held on Mondays when Parliament was sitting. Regular

OVERLEAF: _Entrance Front. The gate tower is the principal surviving feature of Henry VIII's time. The large window to the right lights the Chapel Royal, which Pyne does not illustrate. Built by Henry VIII in the 1530s, the chapel underwent internal refitting by Smirke three centuries later. Queen Victoria's wedding was celebrated in it with some magnificence in February 1840._ View by C. Wild.

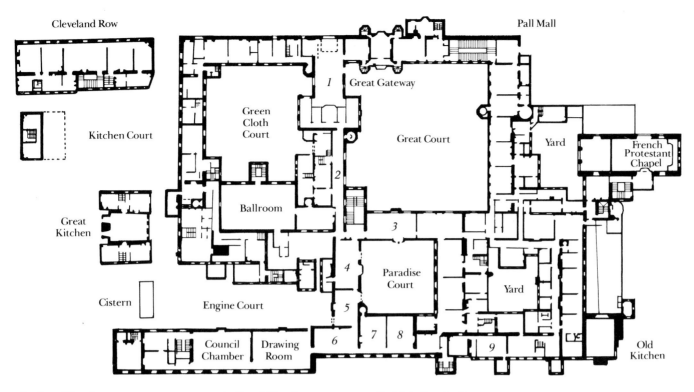

Cleveland Row

Kitchen Court

Great Kitchen

Cistern

Engine Court

Green Cloth Court

1 Great Gateway

Ballroom

2

Great Court

Yard

3

Paradise Court

4

5

Yard

6 *7* *8*

9

Council Chamber | Drawing Room

Pall Mall

French Protestant Chapel

Old Kitchen

1 Chapel Royal
2 Gallery
3 Prince of Wales's Guard Chamber

4 Guard Chamber
5 Presence Chamber
6 Privy Chamber

7 Little Drawing Room
8 State Bedchamber
9 King's Bedchamber

St. James's Palace. First floor plan in 1729.
(Adapted from P.R.O., Works 34/121, 122,
as reproduced in Colvin, ed.,
History of the King's Works, V, 1976.)

10   0   Scale of Metres   50   50   0   Scale of Feet   150

OPPOSITE: *Queen's Library. Here, in a detail*
from the plate on page 56, we see a portion of
the 4,500 volumes that Queen Caroline collected
in her library at St. James's Palace.

Queen's Levee Room. The figure in this detail
from the plate on page 55 shows how Princess
(later Queen) Anne's Little Drawing Room, with
its external staircase, served as a garden room.

attendance in court dress was expected from leading figures in public life. Failure to attend on the part of a Member of Parliament would indicate that he was about to go into opposition. In theory, anyone could be presented to the sovereign on these occasions, provided he found someone willing to present him and could afford court dress. The monarch also transacted official business at levees, held investitures, distributed offices, and received addresses and petitions.

Drawing rooms, attended by both the King and Queen, were open to both sexes and took place on Thursdays and Sundays. They continued well into the nineteenth century, only to be discontinued by Queen Victoria following the death of Prince Albert in 1861. The ceremony associated with levees and drawing rooms survives today in the regular audiences the Prime Minister has with the Queen, in the royal investitures, in the reception of Ambassadors, and in the garden parties given by the Queen at Buckingham Palace and Holyrood House.

In January 1809 a fire destroyed the whole south-east angle of the palace, including the east side of Paradise Court, the adjacent courtyard, and Pheasant Court. Pyne lamented, rightly enough, that these were 'the most ancient and picturesque parts containing the king's and queen's private apartments'. The damaged sections remained unrepaired until 1821, so that when Pyne's artists painted their watercolours this area was a heap of ruins. Court ceremonies had been transferred to Carlton House and, until Queen Charlotte's death in November 1818, to Buckingham House. Pyne evidently found it difficult to find anything very complimentary to say about St. James's Palace, and he gives virtually no proper descriptions of the interiors.

Guard Chamber. This is the first room in the State Apartment formed by Wren for Queen Anne. Yeomen of the Guard are shown warming themselves before a substantial coal fire. The windows look east into Paradise (now Friary) Court, while through the open door in the north wall we can see the staircase leading down to the Great (now Colour) Court. The weapons were displayed decoratively in the customary seventeenth-century fashion, but subsequently, in 1866–67, William Morris & Co. refitted the room in a somewhat gloomy fashion, a commission that would seem surprising for the Socialist Morris. View by C. Wild.

St. James's Palace 53

Old Bedchamber. *The room was the easternmost in Wren's State Apartment, to the immediate east of which lay the interiors destroyed in the fire of 1809. Pyne romantically shows the room furnished with the bed in which Prince James, the son of the ill-fated James II, was born. He explains that at the time of writing the bed belonged to Sir George Osborn, Bt., who housed it at Chicksands Priory, Bedfordshire, in a room imitated from 'the chapter house' at Peterborough Cathedral. The bed, cut down and given a different backcloth decoration, was acquired by the Victoria and Albert Museum from the Trustees of the Osborn Estate and is now displayed in the Queen's bedroom at Kensington Palace.* View by C. Wild.

Queen's Levee Room. This is the Little Drawing Room in the south front of the palace that was fitted up in 1696–97 for Princess Anne, the future Queen, and her husband, Prince George of Denmark. The westernmost window served as a door giving access to an external staircase leading down to the garden, which is clearly shown in Kip's perspective view of the palace in the Britannia Illustrata of 1708. Pyne found the room uncarpeted, although the windows were hung with fashionable festoon curtains in a soft red colour. View by C. Wild.

Queen's Library. Queen Caroline had this exceptionally handsome neo-Palladian room built in 1736–37 from designs by William Kent. Sadly, she died in November of the year it was completed and thus did not live to enjoy the new library. Little used after her death, the space had become a lumber room by 1795, and in 1825 the whole thing would be demolished to make way for York (today Lancaster) House. Kent's chimney-pieces in the style of Inigo Jones were then transferred to the State Apartments at St. James's Palace, where they can now be seen in the Entree and Throne Rooms. The library was adorned with a pair of busts of George II and Queen Caroline by Rysbrack, one at each end of the room, as well as eight busts of poets and philosophers between the arched recesses. The royal busts survive at Windsor Castle. A double cube, 60 by 30 feet, the room was part library and part garden room, with steps leading down into what is now the garden of Lancaster House.

With its 4,500 finely bound books, the Queen's Library was a striking, if today little remembered, tribute to the literary interests of George II's consort. View by C. Wild.

OPPOSITE: *The German Chapel.* Properly known as the Queen's Chapel, this exquisite structure was built by Inigo Jones in 1623–25 for Charles I's wife, Queen Henrietta Maria, who worshipped in the Catholic rite. Fortunately, the fire of 1809 did not touch it, but merely isolated the chapel from the palace so that it now seems to be part of Marlborough House. Important as one of the earliest monuments of Renaissance architecture in England, it was enriched for Charles II in 1682 by Grinling Gibbons, who carved the coat of arms of Catharine of Braganza over the east window. Supported by flying angels from whom depend two great festoons, the composition impales the Stuart arms with those of Portugal. View by C. Wild.

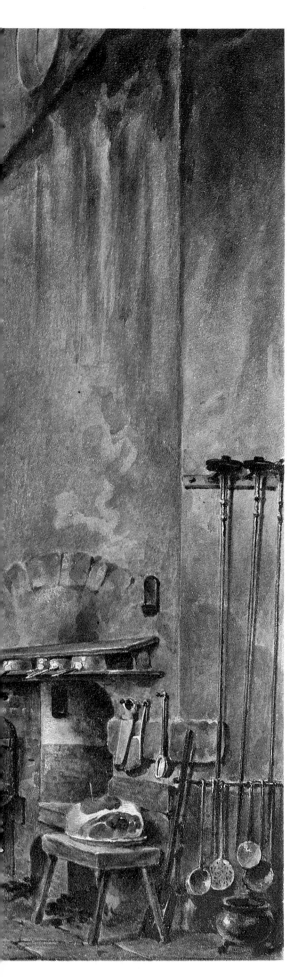

Kitchen. Pyne occasionally takes a rest from rooms of state and shows us behind the scenes. Not that this interior is exactly typical of servants' quarters, for, having almost certainly been designed by Sir John Vanbrugh, the room is of considerable architectural consequence. Built in 1717–19 at a cost of £2,076, the kitchen was intended to serve the apartments of the Prince and Princess of Wales, the future George II and Queen Caroline, who were keeping a more colourful court than the King. But relations between George I and his son had reached their coolest at this time, with the result that in December 1717 the Prince found himself banned from St. James's Palace, and his noble kitchen turned over to the monarch's own purposes. It still survives on the south side of Ambassadors' Court at the west end of the palace. View by J. Stephanoff.

four
Kensington Palace

Pyne's views of Kensington Palace include interiors that are among the very few commissioned by King George I, who had only minimal interest in architecture and court ceremonial. The palace originated as a Jacobean villa that William III bought from the Earl of Nottingham in 1689 with the intention of using it as a simple suburban retreat. During the next forty years, William III and George I enlarged the palace in a confused and haphazard manner that forms a striking contrast to the palaces of the absolutist monarchs of the Continent. One of the most ambitious additions was the new south front, or King's Gallery, designed by Sir Christopher Wren in the first building phase of 1689–96. Under Queen Anne, attention moved to the gardens, where the principal architectural adornment became the magnificent orangery or greenhouse north-east of the palace. Designed by Vanbrugh in 1704–05 in his most monumental manner, the greenhouse survives unaltered. In 1718 Vanbrugh presented George I with an impressive scheme for rebuilding the entire palace in a manner reminiscent of Blenheim, but the King chose merely to add a suite of three new rooms to the existing State Apartments and to employ Kent to redecorate the others.

George I and George II seem to have used the palace as a summer residence, although the latter spent every alternate summer in Hanover and disliked having to return to England. His wife, Queen Caroline, 'made a rule', according to Pyne, 'to hold a public court at Kensington Palace every day after divine service,

OVERLEAF: *Kensington Palace from the south-west. The long range of buildings on the left, the Stone Gallery wing, was built for William III in 1689 as part of the earliest campaign in the gradual enlargement of Nottingham House. It underwent internal reconstruction following a serious fire in November 1691. The gatehouse of 1689, with its crowning clock tower, shown on the extreme left in Westall's view, survives today as the entrance to Great, or Clock, Court. The tall eleven-bay block to the right of the Stone Gallery is the King's Gallery range, built in 1695 by Sir Christopher Wren and still the palace's most architecturally significant façade. An early example of a classical front carried out entirely in brick, it reduces the orders to simple pilaster strips and allows for little ornament save that in the four stone urns on the attic, carved by Caius Gabriel Cibber. The vane just visible on the skyline, and still there, is that of William III's wind dial over the central chimney-piece in the King's Gallery (p. 72). On the extreme right in Westall's view we can see the east front with the pedimented centre-piece built in 1718–19. The three central windows on the first floor belong to the King's Great Drawing Room. View by W. Westall.*

The King's Great Drawing Room. A detail from the plate on page 70, with its view into the Cupola Room and the Privy Chamber beyond, demonstrates how the presence of figures provides the viewer with a sense of the State Rooms' vast scale.

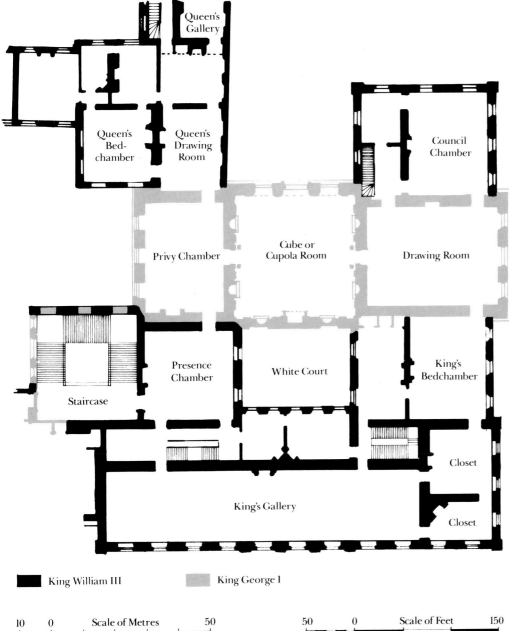

Kensington Palace. The State Apartments.
(Adapted from Colvin, ed.,
History of the King's Works, V, 1976.)

Queen's
Gallery

Queen's
Bed-
chamber

Queen's
Drawing
Room

Council
Chamber

Privy Chamber

Cube or
Cupola Room

Drawing Room

Presence
Chamber

White Court

King's
Bedchamber

Staircase

Closet

King's Gallery

Closet

King William III   King George I

10   0   Scale of Metres   50   50   0   Scale of Feet   150

during his majesty's absence in his Germanic dominions'. An enthusiastic gardener, Queen Caroline employed Wise and Bridgeman to extend the gardens by taking over part of Hyde Park, where Bridgeman created the Serpentine in 1730–32 as the earliest of the many pieces of irregular ornamental water that were to be such a feature of English eighteenth-century parks. The gardens near the palace were enlivened, according to Pyne, with 'a great number of beautiful land tortoises', which had been given to Queen Caroline by the Doge of Genoa. The Serpentine, Round Pond, and radiating avenues survive as memorials to the patronage of George II and his consort.

To Pyne, Kensington Palace, as it stood in 1819, presented a problem. The principal rooms had not been used for over half a century, while the irregular plan and frowsty old-fashioned apartments made it seem to him 'a reproach to English taste'. The central difficulty lay in the work carried out by William Kent during the 1720s for George I. Kent was an indifferent painter in an Italianate seventeenth-century manner, and his approach to the language of classicism, as revealed in the interiors he decorated, seemed slapdash to the Regency eyes of Pyne. Thus, the publisher wrote that the Cupola Room, 'although inspiring in effect from its picturesque style and ponderous decoration, is yet a monument of the bad taste of that age, wherein the usual order of ornament is inverted; for, instead of meeting with marble statues in niches with golden ornaments, we find marble niches containing golden statues'. The room, however, was designed for receptions in the evening when candlelight must have brought its ornament to glittering life. Anyone who has seen a spacious interior lit entirely by candles, even in large chandeliers, will know that the illumination can be surprisingly dim. This may account for the bright colours popular for both clothes and interior decoration during much of the eighteenth century.

George II was the last King to live at Kensington Palace, and on his death in 1760 the building became an architectural and social backwater, described by the topographer Lysons in 1795 as 'entirely forsaken'.[3] The State Apartments thus survive as a fascinating record of the tastes of William III and George I.

OPPOSITE: *Great Staircase. Wren's staircase, with its marble steps and its rich wrought-iron balustrade by Jean Tijou, was constructed in 1696. Some thirty years later William Kent decorated the walls and ceiling with paintings on canvas at a cost of £500. In an illusionistic Venetian Baroque style, these represent on the north and east walls an arcaded loggia filled with members of the court, including the King's dwarf, Ulrich, 'Peter the Wild Boy', and two Turkish Grooms of the Chamber, Mahomet and Mustapha. The* trompe l'oeil *ceiling simulates an open dome from which further spectators look down, including William Kent and an actress commonly regarded as his mistress. The effect of the dome fails to convince, and the staircase generally seems too low for the amount of ornament it contains. The six lanterns shown by Pyne were bought in 1729 but have since disappeared, as has the bizarre green stove-pipe capped with an incongruously elegant neo-classical urn. View by C. Wild.*

The King's Gallery. A detail of the plate on page 72–73 provides a closer view of Sebastiano Ricci's Adoration of the Magi *and the table garniture of Oriental ceramic, the latter so characteristic of the eighteenth-century taste for Chinoiserie.*

Presence Chamber. The carving by Grinling Gibbons on the overmantel survives from the room built by Wren, as does the cornice, but in 1724 William Kent inserted the present doorcases and, more importantly, painted the ceiling in what was described at the time as 'grotesque painting'—that is, in the neo-antique decorative style of Raphael in the Vatican logge, which Kent would have seen during his long stay in Rome.

Pyne explains that this is a 'similar style of decoration to some of the chambers of Herculaneum and Pompeii', and that Kent was 'the first who endeavoured to restore architecture to its ancient style of simplicity and beauty'. Kent is known to have painted the ceilings of the King's Bedchamber and the Council Chamber in the same style, but these works, executed in 1723–24, do not survive. Stephanoff's view shows how George III crowded the walls with a great variety of paintings, some hung on top of tapestry. Facing each other are two enormous cartoons painted in the 1670s by the Bolognese artist Carlo Cignani (1628–1719) for the fresco decorations in the Palazzo del Giardino in Parma. On the left hangs Europa and the Bull and on the right Bacchus and Ariadne. Two of a set of seven acquired by George III from the Smith collection in 1763, the cartoons have been displayed since 1835 at Hampton Court. View by J. Stephanoff.

———————

BELOW: *Queen Caroline's Drawing Room.* Originally the Privy Chamber, this room is the first of the three that were added to the State Apartments in 1718–19 for George I by an unknown architect, perhaps Colen Campbell. In 1723 William Kent painted the oval centre-piece of the ceiling, a scene of Minerva surrounded by the Arts and Sciences rendered in a somewhat enervated Baroque style. He doubtless also designed the elaborate carved- and gilt-wood dolphin side-tables seen here between the windows but now removed to Windsor. View by C. Wild.

Cupola Room. The Cube or Cupola Room, the central feature of the three rooms added in 1718–19, provided an unusual forecast of the neo-antique effects that were to be popular later in the century. One contemporary described the Cube Room, with its giant Ionic pilasters, as 'exactly done according to the Grecian taste'.[4] *However, the coffering on the ceiling cove is not real but, rather, painted in* trompe l'oeil. *William Kent received £350 for the work in 1722 and over £350 in 1724–25 for further* trompe l'oeil *paintings on the walls. Pyne remarks tartly that the room conforms with 'the general style of that period, which aimed at an appearance of splendour at small expense'. The four brass chandeliers on purple ropes and the Kentian sphinx tables no longer stand in the room, but Rysbrack's* Roman Marriage, *a bas-relief over the chimney, survives, as does the enormous central clock, which, made by Charles Clay and completed by Charles Pyke in 1743, once belonged to Augusta, Princess of Wales, mother of George III. It contained a mechanism for playing airs by Handel and has a cupola adorned with bronze figures by Roubiliac.* View by G. Cattermole.

The King's Great Drawing Room. This is the last and easternmost of the three new rooms, built in 1718–19, and in Pyne's view we look west from it across the Cupola Room to the Privy Chamber, later Queen Caroline's Drawing Room. In 1722–23 Kent painted the oval centre of the ceiling with an ambitious mythological group, representing Jupiter and Semele, which was being dismantled in 1819 but has since been reinstated. Kent also designed the picture frames, the mirrors and the elaborate sculptural chimney-piece, carved by James Richards in 1724.

Pyne claims that the room was an early instance of 'the then new art of paper-hangings, in imitation of the old velvet flock'. Wallpaper of this kind had first come into popularity at the end of the seventeenth century, so that Kent's use of it in the 1720s was not a total novelty. The great paintings facing each other had been commissioned in 1742 from John Wootton by Frederick, Prince of Wales. They depict the sieges of Tournay and Lille, scenes from Marlborough's campaigns against Louis XIV. George III had hung them in the Great Drawing Room, but in 1822 the

pictures were removed to St. James's Palace, where they remain. View by C. Wild.

OPPOSITE ABOVE: *Queen's Private Dining Room.* With its deep brown wainscoting, its door panels grained as walnut, its chairs in rich crimson velvet and its Kentian sphinx table, this is a warm and rich little room. For Queen Caroline, William Kent had hung the walls with the royal collection of portraits of early Kings. The room was unfortunately reduced in size in 1899. View by J. Stephanoff.

RIGHT: _Queen's Gallery. Running north from the main body of the palace, the wing containing this gallery was built in 1690–91 as an addition to the Queen's Apartment. The overmantel mirror carved by Grinling Gibbons survives from that time, but his four mirrors over the doors, two of which are shown in Stephanoff's view, have since disappeared. Copies of two of them were introduced when the room was restored and redecorated in c. 1970. Queen Mary had died in the adjoining bedroom in 1694. The Gallery was subsequently painted white and gilded, probably in c. 1735 by Queen Caroline, for whom the organ case at the far end was made. In 1763 Queen Charlotte had William Vile transform the organ case into a cupboard. In the same year he provided the mahogany pedestal cupboards, in which the Queen probably kept her collection of prints and drawings. She hung the gallery with a set of full-length royal portraits,_

including the painting of Henry VIII, after Holbein, shown on the extreme left. An architectural feature to be noted here and throughout Wren's interiors at Kensington Palace is the extreme lowness of the dado rail. The intention may have been to increase the apparent height of the rooms, or to compensate for the low stature of William III. In the centre of the room is a musical clock by Charles Clay. View by J. Stephanoff.

The King's Gallery. Built by Wren in 1695–96 as a picture gallery, this room was completely redecorated by Kent in 1725–27 at a cost of £500. Kent designed the chimney-pieces, door-cases, pedestals, and side-tables; he also painted and gilded the wainscot, which may originally have been only varnished and grained. In addition, the crimson curtains of cut wool velvet appear to date from the time of Kent. The principal glory of the room is that artist's ceiling painted on canvas with scenes from the Odyssey framed in scrolls and arabesques on a gold ground simulating mosaic. Over the chimney-piece is William III's celebrated wind dial painted in c. 1696 by Robert Norden and gilded by René Cousin. It elicited considerable admiration from Peter the Great during a private visit to King William in 1698. At the far end of the room Pyne shows Sebastiano Ricci's great Adoration of the Magi, *a work of 1726. Acquired by George III from Joseph Smith in 1763, the painting hangs today at Hampton Court. By the time Pyne's aquatint was published in October 1816, the paintings had already been removed from the King's Gallery at Kensington. In the 1730s the great space was cut up into three smaller rooms for the use of the heiress presumptive, Princess Victoria, but it has since been reinstated.* View by C. Wild.

five
Buckingham House

When Pyne visited Buckingham House the interiors were an untouched example of the taste of George III and Queen Charlotte at the start of their reign. Towards the end of the century the royal couple spent less time there and more at Kew and Windsor, so that the Buckingham House interiors, like so many in Pyne's *Royal Residences*, were beginning to be seen as an historical period piece. Within ten years they had all been completely transformed by Nash's more meretricious style. Thus, Pyne's record came in the nick of time.

Since the fire at Whitehall Palace in 1698, the modest and irregular Tudor buildings of St. James's Palace had served as the London residence of the monarch and as the seat of the court, which it technically remains today. George III, on ascending the throne in 1760 at the age of twenty-two, did not want to live in any of the palaces associated with his grandfather George II, especially Hampton Court and Kensington, and least of all in St. James's Palace, which he once described as 'this dust trap'. In 1762 the young King bought Buckingham House for £28,000 from the illegitimate son of the last Duke of Buckingham. It now became known as the Queen's House and indeed was transferred to Queen Charlotte by Act of Parliament in 1775 in exchange for Somerset House in the Strand, which had been the traditional dower house of English Queens. George III and Queen Charlotte moved into Buckingham House during the summer of 1762, bringing furniture and pictures from Hampton Court and Kensington Palace. Thereafter they used St. James's Palace only for court ceremonies such as levees, drawing rooms, balls, royal marriages, and christenings. The author of a recent biography of George III claims that in thus dividing his time between the two buildings, this sovereign 'was the first British monarch to make a distinction between his court and his home, between his public and his private

OVERLEAF: *Buckingham House, east front. Built in 1702–05 for the first Duke of Buckingham by Winde and Talman, Buckingham House was one of the earliest examples in England of a type that subsequently became familiar, a type in which quadrant colonnades were linked by flanking stable wings to form a forecourt. The few seventeenth-century precedents included Inigo Jones's Stoke Bruerne, Northamptonshire, and Hugh May's Berkeley House, Piccadilly. The building that Westall shows, although completely remodelled by Nash, still forms the core of the present-day Buckingham Palace. However, in the 1760s George III had employed Sir William Chambers to simplify its design as part of his bid for an unobtrusive manner of living. Thus, by Pyne's day Buckingham House had lost its angle pilasters and its statues on the skyline. Moreover, the open arcades in the stable wings had been filled in, and, saddest of all, the forecourt had lost its Baroque fountain, as well as its handsome gates and curved railings by Tijou.* View by W. Westall.

Staircase. A detail, from the plate on page 81, of Wyatt's Corinthian colonnade leading to the central flight of the grand staircase built in 1800.

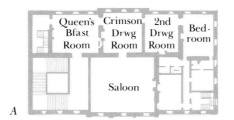

Queen's Bfast Room	Crimson Drwg Room	2nd Drwg Room	Bed-room

Saloon

A

Buckingham House. A. The first floor in 1762. B. The ground floor with additions made by George III. (Adapted from Colvin, ed., History of the King's Works, V, 1976.)

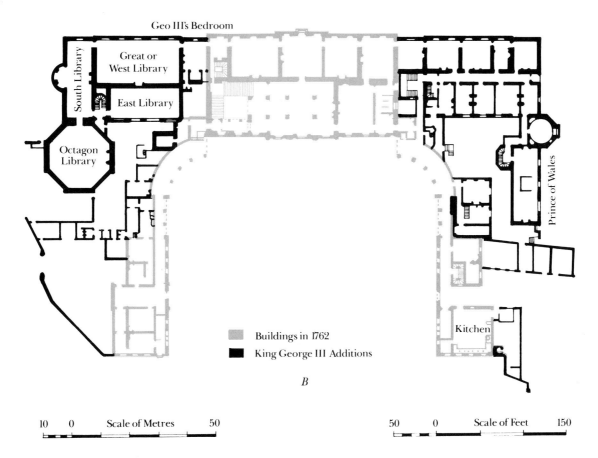

Geo III's Bedroom

South Library

Great or West Library

East Library

Octagon Library

Prince of Wales

Kitchen

■ Buildings in 1762

■ King George III Additions

B

10   0   Scale of Metres   50

50   0   Scale of Feet   150

life. St. James's became the King's place of business; his London home was the Queen's House'.[5]

Buckingham House was a private palace built in 1702–05 by William Winde, but probably designed by William Talman, for John Sheffield, first Duke of Buckingham. Its numerous Baroque features did not please the young George III, who had been tutored in architecture by the fashionable neo-classical architect, William Chambers. In 1761 the King created the new royal office of Architect of Works, a post that would be shared by Chambers and his great rival Robert Adam. Chambers was given the task of remodelling Buckingham House in 1762–69 in a simple neo-classical taste, which meant stripping the place of some of its Baroque flourishes. Thus, Pyne wrote of the King's private apartments on the ground floor at the back that their decoration was plain in character, like the King himself, and that the 'ornaments selected by this virtuous sovereign are such as change not with the fashions of the times'. Pyne does not illustrate any of the monarch's private rooms, except for two of the four sparsely

Saloon. A detail, from the plate on page 82, of Chambers's neo-classical wall, Robert Adams's chimney-piece, and John Bacon the Elder's clock, the later two features now in the Queen's Presence Chamber at Windsor Castle.

ornamented libraries designed by Chambers to keep pace with the growth of his patron's bibliomania, although the interest was more in collecting than in reading books.

Chambers left the original staircase largely intact, with its magnificent Baroque wall paintings by Laguerre, although he altered the north landing so as to allow access to the Queen's Saloon or Throne Room. The rich decoration of the Queen's private apartments, situated on the first floor, was in striking contrast to that of the King's rooms. An informed and enthusiastic collector and connoisseur, the consort gave rise to interiors at Buckingham House that are an impressive tribute to her taste. They were also the scene of a warm and gay family life, a life happily recorded in the charming conversation pieces that Zoffany painted of the Queen and her children at Buckingham House in the 1760s. Mrs. Lybbe Powys, on a visit in 1767, recorded that, 'tho' but in March, every room was full of roses, carnations, hyacinths, &c., dispersed in the prettiest manner imaginable in jars and different flower-pots on stands … we were amazed to find so large a house so warm, but fires, it seems, are kept the whole day, even in the closets, and to prevent accidents to furniture…there is in every chimney a lacquered wire fire-board'.[6]

From the moment Queen Charlotte died in 1818, the Prince Regent had an eye on his mother's mansion as a possible future residence for himself. When Nash drew up plans for remodelling it in 1825, the Prince, who had become George IV in 1820, envisaged Buckingham House as a grandiose *pied-à-terre,* but while construction work proceeded, probably in December 1826, he decided to make it the ceremonial centre of his court. Nash protested in vain that his building provided neither for a Queen nor for the Lord Chamberlain's or Lord Steward's departments. All Nash could do was increase the decorative richness of his reception rooms and heighten his new wings flanking the forecourt, which had already been criticized as inadequate on aesthetic grounds. Nash in 1827 was seventy-five years old and his royal patron exactly a decade younger. The palace they created was the exuberant culmination of the francophile tastes they had shared during their long careers. Architecturally, Nash's work reflected a range of Parisian neo-classical monuments, such as Gabriel's palaces in the Place de la Concorde (1755) and Rousseau's Hôtel de Salm (1786), while the placing of the Marble Arch (removed to Hyde Park in 1851) in front of Buckingham Palace echoed the relation of Percier and Fontaine's Arc du Carrousel (1806–07) to the Tuileries Palace.

Inside, Nash destroyed or remodelled every interior shown by Pyne to create a resplendant sequence of State Apartments in a combination of Rococo, Louis XVI, and French Empire styles. Their magnificence gave tangible expression to the mood of a nation flushed with victory over Napoleon and enriched by the fruits of the Industrial Revolution. Nonetheless, Nash's prediction that the building would be inadequate was soon proved right, for twice it had to be extended, first by Blore in the 1830s and 1840s and then by Pennethorne in the 1850s. Yet it is still Nash's interiors that, with minor modifications by Blore, form the setting for the ceremonies of the most splendid royal court to survive in the modern world.

The King's Octagon Library. This detail, from the plate on page 84, evinces George III's typically eighteenth-century passion for books.

Staircase from the Grand Hall. Wyatt's staircase of 1800 took the place of the original staircase that Winde had installed in 1702 with a balustrade by Tijou. Wyatt adopted the so-called 'imperial' type—that is, rising in a central flight and returning in two against the side walls—whereas Winde's more modest staircase had followed the outer walls of the stair hall. Wyatt introduced the handsome screen of Corinthian columns and the bold Palladian arches supporting the side flights. However, all this splendour survived for only twenty-five years before it would be replaced by Nash. In Wyatt's day, as now, the entrance hall or Grand Hall retained the comparatively modest size and low proportions of the original interior designed by Winde. Here George III hung sixteen of the paintings by Canaletto that he had bought from Consul Joseph Smith in 1763. One of these, a view of the Pantheon, can just be seen on the extreme right in Cattermole's view. Below it is a 1766 painting by Visentini and Zuccarelli, entitled Triumphal Arch to George II _and also_

acquired from Joseph Smith. Both paintings are today at Windsor Castle. View by G. Cattermole.

OPPOSITE: _Staircase._ The sumptuous Baroque paintings of c. 1705 on the walls and ceiling were the masterpiece of Louis Laguerre, who had been a pupil of Le Brun. Born at Versailles, where Louis XIV was his godfather, Laguerre came to England in c. 1684 and worked under Verrio at Windsor Castle. The destruction of the staircase paintings, which depicted Dido and Aeneas, must be regarded as a major tragedy, carried out by Nash in the 1820s. The actual staircase shown in Stephanoff's view is not the original one with a balustrade by Tijou, but a flight inserted by James Wyatt in 1800 and based on a 1776 design by Chambers. Nash replaced the whole arrangement— paintings, railings, and all—with a showy design of his own. View by J. Stephanoff.

Saloon. *Chambers introduced a doorway on the north landing of the Laguerre staircase to enable visitors to pass directly into the Queen's Saloon at the centre of the east front. He reconstructed the two-storeyed saloon of the original mansion, replacing its rich Laguerre wall frescoes with a delicate neo-classical scheme consisting of pilaster strips painted with arabesques, similar to the arrangement in James Stuart's Painted Room of 1758 at Spencer House, and with Cipriani's grisaille bas-reliefs styled all'antica. In the years 1763–87 the Raphael Cartoons from Hampton Court hung in this room; thus, Chambers's decorative wall treatment, illustrated by Pyne, may not have been carried out in the 1760s but only after the*

cartoons had been removed. *The chimney-piece, for example, was designed by Robert Adam and carries a marble clock with figures of Vigilance and Patience carved by John Bacon the Elder in 1789. Both chimney-piece and clock are today in the Queen's Presence Chamber at Windsor Castle. Pyne also shows Queen Charlotte's chair of state and crimson-velvet canopy, for later in her reign she held her drawing rooms here rather than at St. James's Palace. In 1799 the room was refurnished with William Adair's elaborate gilt pelmets and sofas, their coverings and cushions of white cotton velvet painted with flowers by Princess Elizabeth. These had disappeared by the time Stephanoff painted his watercolour.*

Second Drawing Room.   This lay immediately north of the Crimson Drawing Room and boasted a similarly splendid painted ceiling, the work of Chambers and Cipriani. Fitted with wall hangings of a deeper colour than those in the Crimson Drawing Room, the Second Drawing Room also contained masterpieces of Baroque painting. Both rooms lacked a carpet, since they were intended for large receptions. At the centre of the left wall was van Dyck's The Villiers Boys, *while over the chimney-piece hung his no less celebrated triple portrait,* The Three Eldest Children of Charles I. *Both paintings are now at Windsor Castle, where the chimney-piece itself is also to be found in the State Bedroom. View by J. Stephanoff.*

The King's Octagon Library. This remarkable two-storeyed room was built in 1766–67 from designs by Sir William Chambers at the east end of the South Library to house the collection of books that George III had bought in 1763 from Joseph Smith, British Consul in Venice. The room looks oddly like the Georgianized chapter house of a medieval cathedral, for example that at Westminster Abbey before Sir Gilbert Scott's restoration in 1864–65. The four-sided astronomical clock on the central octagonal desk was made for the King in 1765 by Eardley Norton at a cost of £1,042. It survives today at Buckingham Palace, complete with the mahogany case and openwork silver panels. View by J. Stephanoff.

The Queen's Breakfast Room. Immediately south of the Crimson Drawing Room, the Breakfast Room was one of the most interesting interiors at Buckingham House illustrated by Pyne. When Queen Charlotte turned the Duke of Buckingham's Japan Room into the Crimson Drawing Room, she brought its black and gold lacquer panels to her Breakfast Room next door. The work of repairing the panels and making new ones to fit the new room was executed by the royal cabinet-maker William Vile, who charged the substantial sum of £572.12s. This shows the importance attached to a room that may well have been the finest example in England of the sort of japanned chinoiserie interiors so familiar on the Continent. However, the description left by a visitor in 1802 makes the room seem somewhat dowdy, with its brown and maroon curtains, painted in imitation of cut velvet by Princess Elizabeth, and its bare, carpetless floor. Since that date, however, it evidently had been spruced up with characteristic Regency curtains in red with black trimmings, matching case-covers for the chairs, and a red carpet with a gold pattern, probably of Brussels weave. The pedimented mirrors between the windows dated from c. 1740, but the organ,

crowned with a bust of Handel, had been supplied by Bradburn in 1767. View by G. Cattermole.

ABOVE: _Blue Velvet Room._ This room and the Queen's Breakfast Room, intended for the consort's private use, were richly carpeted. The King always eschewed carpets, believing, no doubt rightly, that they harboured dust. With its Lely portraits and its landscapes by Claude and both the Poussins, the Blue Velvet Room illustrates the care taken in the eighteenth century to harmonize colours and fabrics throughout an interior. Thus, the walls were hung with light-blue silk and the chairs and sofa covered in velvet of the same hue. A darker blue, combined with gold, served for the curtains as well as for the chandelier sleeve. Between the windows can be seen a pair of Derbyshire Bluejohn, or fluorspar, candelabra and vases. Still in the Royal Collection, these are part of an elegantly neo-classical garniture de cheminée, including a clock, made for King George III and Queen Charlotte in c. 1770 by Matthew Boulton from designs by Sir William Chambers. View by C. Wild.

six

Frogmore House

Here is yet another royal residence for which Pyne's watercolours form a unique record of interiors that were shortly to be completely remodelled. It was in 1790 that Queen Charlotte bought the lease of Frogmore, a small house and estate on crown land about a mile and a half south-east of Windsor Castle. She would make it her Petit Trianon, a place to escape from court life at Windsor and to decorate as she wished. In 1791 the Queen invited the architect James Wyatt to Gothicize the late-seventeenth-century house, which had probably been designed by Hugh May. Eventually, however, she settled on an elegant neo-classical design, which Wyatt executed in 1792–95. He added another storey to the centre block and flanking pavilions with bowed centres linked along the whole west front, its open Doric colonnade, now glazed, rather like that at his contemporary Stoke Park, Buckinghamshire. The Queen landscaped the park, embellishing it with an ornamental lake from designs by the Vice Chamberlain of her household, Major William Price, brother of Sir Uvedale Price, the great theorist of the Picturesque.

OVERLEAF: *Frogmore House, exterior view. In what she called 'my little paradise',*[7] *Queen Charlotte and her numerous unmarried daughters spent their days gardening, drawing, and studying botany. The garden front of the sparklingly elegant house, rebuilt for her by James Wyatt in 1792–95, survives today exactly as in the watercolour painted for Pyne by C. Wild.*

Red Japan Room. A detail, from the plate on page 97, showing 'the imitation of rich japan' painted by George III's daughter Princess Elizabeth.

The Green Pavilion. This detail, from the plate on page 96, gives a view into Queen Charlotte's beloved light- and air-filled loggia.

Frogmore thus became the model neo-classical villa of the type that every Regency man of taste longed to own. Indeed, so many people wanted to see it that the Queen opened the house by ticket to 'respectable parties'. Pyne's six delectable watercolour views form not the least charming part of the whole three volumes of *Royal Residences*. Sadly, Her Majesty had died the autumn before the record of the house was published, although Pyne describes how she gave many fêtes in the Frogmore grounds not only to the royal family and the nobility but also 'to neighbouring gentry and even to tradesmen and their families and others in the middle sphere of society'. The house was ready by her birthday in May 1795, when George III's consort gave a fête at which she set up on the lawns the tent captured from Tipoo Sahib at Seringapatam. Guests were entertained by tumblers and 'a Dutch wake'. In July 1817, the year before she died, Queen Charlotte gave a great garden party to the boys of Eton, always a favourite with her husband, at which 2,000 guests enjoyed the 'animated huzzas of these youths' as they played cricket and disported themselves in the 'asiatic tents'.

Library. In this detail, from the plate on page 95, we see the elegance with which the windows were treated in Queen Charlotte's library at Frogmore.

OPPOSITE: *Green Closet. This room had a red fitted carpet, and, in contrast to the Red Japan Room (p. 97), its walls were hung with 'original japan, of a beautiful fabric, on a plain pure ground'.[8] The cabinet and chairs were made of Indian cane. The full history of orientalizing décor in the eighteenth century, which seems to have been a characteristically royal taste, has yet to be written.* View by C. Wild.

At Frogmore the Queen kept her botanical collections, printing press, and a large part of her library, while her talented daughter, Princess Elizabeth, passed much of her time in painting activity that included the simulated lacquer panels shown in Wild's watercolour of the Red Japan Room (p. 97). He curiously does not illustrate the room in the south pavilion that was decorated by Mary Moser (1744–1819), the leading professional flower painter of her day. The drawing mistress of Queen Charlotte's daughters, Miss Moser became Mrs. Hugh Lloyd in 1784 and was one of the first two women members of the Royal Academy of Arts, founded by George III in 1768. The richly garlanded Miss Moser's Room survives intact, complete with its large-scale flower paintings on black grounds, for which the artist received £900.

Queen Charlotte bequeathed the tenancy of Frogmore to her daughter, Princess Augusta, who lived in it until her death in 1840, when the house passed to the Duchess of Kent, the mother of Queen Victoria. The gardens were redesigned for Queen Mary after the First World War, and the house in its gleaming white stucco survives today as arguably the most attractive of the many royal residences.

Eating Room. The dining room, with its chaste apsidal ends, was in Wyatt's north pavilion. Pyne described it as 'fitted up in a style of elegant simplicity in conformity with the notions of Her Majesty'. The chairs, as always in the eighteenth century when not in use, were ranged round the walls, the latter distempered so as to seal the room against the effluvia of food. The elaborate curtains were predominantly white with a red bobbin fringe and red swags, their colour echoed in the red seats to the chairs. The blue and red carpet picked up the light-blue colour of the walls and the red of the chairs. The walls were hung with a collection of Mecklenburg-Strelitz family portraits suspended on decorative cords. View by C. Wild.

Library. The warm gold-brown colouring of the Queen's library in Wyatt's southern pavilion was in total contrast to the crisp, fresh dining room in the northern pavilion, with its chill blue walls and white woodwork. The bookcases, doors, and shutters in the library were grained in imitation satinwood and the walls painted in a harmonizing shade of brown. Dark-brown mullions and curtains composed of intertwined festoons of a light-brown material and a patterned green brought both elegance and emphasis to the windows. In our present view, black plaster busts of literary figures surmount the bookcases that line every wall. This charming room had a short life in the form seen here, for the Queen's books were sold at Christie's in 1819, following her death in the previous year. View by C. Wild.

The Green Pavilion. This was an engagingly colourful interior, composed of green walls, red curtains with green bobbins, grey dado and door surrounds, brown mullions, and an Adam-style carpet. It opened directly into the loggia that Queen Charlotte described as 'a colonnade the whole length of the house which will make a sweet retirement in the summer all dressed out with Flowers'. View by C. Wild.

OPPOSITE: *Red Japan Room. Pyne records that this room was painted 'in imitation of rich japan by H.R.H. Princess Elizabeth',*

who also ornamented the furniture. The total effect seems a bit
jazzy, with red banquettes round the edge of the room and red
curtains with gold bobbin fringe and blue swags. Of George III's
seven daughters, Princess Elizabeth was one of the three who
managed to break free of the close family circle and marry. This
she did in 1818, at the age of forty-eight, and became the wife of
Landgrave Friedrich of Hesse Homburg. An enthusiastic
architectural patron, Princess Elizabeth employed Georg Moller in
the 1820s to build the Gothic House at Homburg in the English
castle style and to remodel the seventeenth-century Schloss in a
restrained neo-classical mode. View by C. Wild.

seven
*C*arlton *H*ouse

The richness and finesse of the interiors created for the Prince Regent, the future George IV, between 1783 and 1814 made Carlton House one of the finest royal residences anywhere in contemporary Europe. Thus, while the building was modest in size, its demolition in 1826–27 constituted one of the greatest losses in English royal and architectural history. Pyne recognized the importance of Carlton House by devoting no less than twenty-four plates to it, only one fewer than to Windsor itself, three times as many as to St. James's Palace, and over twice as many as to Buckingham House. Within six years of the publication of Pyne's plates, the palace that Horace Walpole predicted in 1785 would 'be the most perfect in Europe',[9] was demolished on the King's order to help pay for the new work at Buckingham Palace. On the site of its gardens Nash built the two handsome Carlton House Terraces in 1827–33, which were rented out, to provide Crown revenue, by the Commissioners of Woods, Forests and Land Revenues. Marlborough House and even St. James's Palace, which George IV proposed to demolish as part of the same redevelopment, were fortunately spared.

The enthusiasm Pyne expresses for Carlton House is related to the fact that, alone out of the royal residences he describes, it was, at the time of writing, the centre of an active court life. Queen Charlotte had died in 1818, while her husband, George III, survived another two years in isolation and near madness at Windsor. Their palaces thus seemed melancholy in contrast to Carlton House, which, moreover, was decorated in a far more up-to-date style. Just as the watercolours of Windsor Castle hold great importance as the only record of the destroyed Baroque interiors by Hugh May, so the Carlton House views provide the only record of Henry Holland's no less important interiors of a century later.

The Carlton House watercolours are singularly fascinating for documenting the changing tastes of the Prince Regent who, by 1819, had altered and refurnished most of Holland's 1780s interiors in an increasingly opulent style. As originally furnished, the residence reflected the francophile tastes of the Prince in his youth, when he employed dealers like Dominique Daguerre to acquire French furniture in a restrained Louis XVI manner. After the

OVERLEAF: *North Front. The entrance front was dominated by a portico of Corinthian columns, perhaps the most sumptuous ever executed in London. They can be seen today, although deprived of their rich frieze and some of the ornamental carving on their capitals, as part of the side porticoes at the National Gallery (1834–38) in Trafalgar Square, where the architect Wilkins was forced to reuse them. In French architectural conventions governing the hierarchy of the classical orders, a Corinthian portico of this kind would be appropriate only for a royal or civic building, not for the private house of an ordinary subject. The portico at Carlton House was an early instance of the* porte-cochère, *which permitted a whole carriage to be driven into it so that members of the household or guests could enter the mansion without ever getting wet.* View by W. Westall.

Ante-Chamber to the Throne Room. A detail, from the plate on page 109, of the opulent, richly gilded Empire-style furniture designed for the Prince Regent.

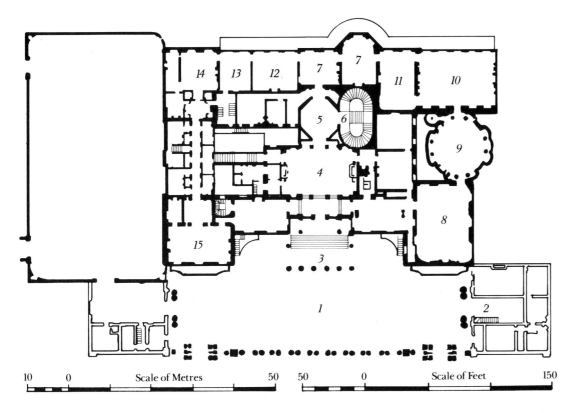

Carlton House. Henry Holland's plan for the principal floor, c. 1790. (Adapted from Robinson, Royal Residences, 1982.)

1   Forecourt
2   Kitchen Wing
3   Portico
4   Hall
5   Octagon
6   Staircase
7   Ante Chambers
8   Grand Eating Room
9   Music Room
10   Great Drawing Room
11   Throne Room
12   Her Royal Highness's
     Private Drawing Room
13   Salon
14   Bedchamber
15   Library

Scale of Metres   10   0   50   Scale of Feet   50   0   150

French Revolution, he developed richer tastes and could now acquire masterpieces of French royal furniture, including sumptuous Boulle pieces, as well as the Dutch cabinet paintings that had often accompanied them. Finally, in the early nineteenth century, he patronized English furniture manufacturers who were moving towards the heavy neo-antique manner with which the name 'Regency' is today often associated. The Prince's constantly changing tastes bewildered his contemporaries. For example, in May 1810 Lady Sarah Spencer visited Carlton House 'which is so magnificent just now.... He changes the furniture so very often, that one can scarcely find time to catch a glimpse of each transient arrangement before it is all turned off for some other'.[10]

We should not forget that the creation of Carlton House was contemporary with that of the fantastic Royal Pavilion at Brighton, built for the Prince Regent in 1786–87 by the same architect, Henry Holland, as a simple neo-classical villa. However, just as John Nash and others had remodelled Carlton House in c. 1813 to keep pace with the Prince's increasingly luxurious tastes, so Nash also transformed the Royal Pavilion into an Oriental extravaganza in 1815–21. And when George IV commissioned the ravishing aquatints in *The Royal Pavilion at Brighton* (1827), he may have been encouraged by the charm of Pyne's *Royal Residences* (1819).

Carlton House, the site of which is today roughly defined by the area between Pall Mall and the Duke of York's column, was a seventeenth-century building acquired in 1732 by Frederick, Prince of Wales, son of George I, who was an enthusiast for exotic styles like Chinoiserie and Rococo as well as for the new art of landscape gardening. He had employed William Kent to lay out a new Picturesque garden every trace of which has disappeared, but its

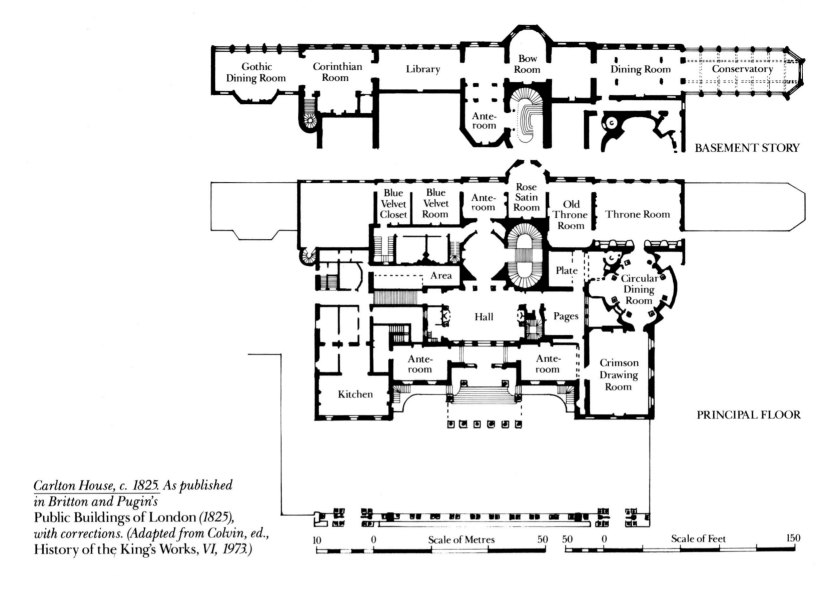

BASEMENT STORY

PRINCIPAL FLOOR

Carlton House, c. 1825. As published
in Britton and Pugin's
Public Buildings of London *(1825),*
with corrections. (Adapted from Colvin, ed.,
History of the King's Works, *VI, 1973.)*

significance in the history of garden design can be appreciated from contemporary engravings and from the following comment in a letter written by Sir Thomas Robinson to Lord Carlisle in December 1734:

There is a new taste in gardening just arisen, which has been practised with so great success at the Prince's garden in Town, that a general alteration of some of the most considerable gardens in the Kingdom is begun, after Mr. Kent's notion of gardening, viz., to lay them out, and work without either level or line...this method of gardening is the more agreeable, as, when finished, it has the appearance of beautiful nature, and without being told, one would imagine art had no part in the finishing, and is, according to what one hears of the Chinese entirely after their models for works of this nature, where they never plant straight lines or make regular designs.

On the death of Prince Frederick in 1751, the house was occupied by his widow Augusta, Dowager Princess of Wales, who employed Sir William Chambers to adorn her celebrated gardens at Kew with exotic Oriental buildings. She may also have had improvements made at Carlton House, possibly even including the garden front with its central canted bay. On her death in 1772 the house remained empty for some years until it was acquired as the town residence of George, Prince of Wales, on his coming of age in 1783. Parliament now voted £60,000 for its rehabilitation, and Chambers, who had been appointed Surveyor General and Comptroller of the King's Works in 1782, undertook some necessary repairs. However, the young Prince regarded the sixty-year-old architect as too much the creature of his father, George III, from whom he was to react both politically and architecturally. He thus chose as his architect the thirty-seven-year-old Henry Holland, whose elegant Brooks's Club in St. James's Street, erected in 1776–78, had so delighted its members that the building established the architect overnight as one of the most sought-after in the country, especially with the Whig aristocrats who frequented the club. The Prince of Wales himself became a member of Brooks's in 1783, and later in the same year he appointed Holland architect for Carlton House. From that time onwards Holland brilliantly remodelled and extended the muddle of buildings that occupied the site, providing a dense network of interlocking rooms of contrasting shapes. The planning recalls that of eighteenth-century town mansions in Paris, especially in its delicate shift in axis between the centre of the entrance front and that of the garden front.

In 1794 Holland closed the forecourt to Pall Mall with an open screen of Greek Ionic columns, a charming idea borrowed from French neo-classical theory and practice. Some of the columns were subsequently re-used by Nash in the conservatories at Buckingham Palace, where they can be seen today. Holland then left the garden front, with its central canted bay, more or less in its Flitcroft form. The site slopes considerably down from Pall Mall towards the Mall, with the result that the garden front was three storeys high as opposed to the two storeys of the entrance front.

By 1785 a substantial amount of work had been completed in the Prince's apartments along the south front. However, progress had now to be halted, a consequence of the appalling debts the Prince had run up following his marriage to Mrs. Fitzherbert in December 1785. Work resumed in 1787, and within two years most of the state rooms in the west and north fronts were complete, although work on the exterior of the north front continued until 1794. The house was ready for the Prince to hold his first state levee on 8 February 1790. This proved to be a dazzling occasion, despite the absence of ladies, owing to the marriage to Mrs. Fitzherbert not being recognized, which made the Prince technically a bachelor. As such, he could hold only levees, which were all male gatherings, and not drawing rooms, which were attended by both sexes.

George IV's barbarous decision to demolish his exquisite miniature palace can never be forgiven. Although its columns were reused at the National Gallery and Buckingham Palace, and some of its doors, chimney-pieces, and parquet floors salvaged for incorporation at Windsor Castle and Buckingham Palace, the ghost of so much vanished magnificence still haunts the eastern end of Pall Mall.

Conservatory, looking west. A detail, from the plate on page 124, of Hopper's tour de force, *a fan-vaulted chamber made entirely of cast-iron and glass.*

Great Hall. *The entrance hall was a spectacular space surrounded on all four sides by open screens of Ionic columns and surmounted by a coffered top-lit ceiling. The mahogany seat furniture, which was probably designed by Holland in 1794, contrasts with the richer gilded furniture that the Prince acquired after Holland's departure in 1802. Although the room seen here survived more completely than any other in its original Holland form, we should note that it had been enriched in 1804 by the painter M.C. Wyatt, who bronzed the mouldings and the capitals of the yellow scagliola columns, marbled the dado in dark-green verd-antique, and painted the walls a light granite green, the latter found as well in the adjacent octagonal tribune and staircase.* View by C. Wild.

OPPOSITE: Staircase. *The arched opening on the left hung with red drapery leads from the ground-floor octagonal vestibule* shown on page 106. *The footman is descending with a tray of delicacies to the lower ground floor. A spectacular spatial composition, the oval staircase can only be described as Baroque. Certainly it owed much to William Kent's 1740s staircase at 44 Berkeley Square, as well as to Chambers's staircases at Somerset House (1776–96). The glazed dome was prettily decorated with painted glass inspired by Raphael's* grotteschi *in the Vatican* logge. *On the half-landing stood a splendid pedestal clock in the full Rococo style of Louis XV. Veneered with tulipwood, purplewood, and mahogany, and decorated with gilt-bronze mounts in the style of Caffieri, it was traditionally made for Versailles. After buying it in 1816 for £262.10s, the Prince Regent placed the clock in the conspicuous position on the staircase, where Pyne would record it. Stamped by François Dahomet, the elegant, 9-foot-high piece today graces one of the interiors at Buckingham Palace.* View by C. Wild.

Vestibule. The entrance hall opened dramatically into the unusual octagonal tribune or vestibule, which provided the pivot on which the whole complex plan revolved. Two-storeyed, the vestibule was surrounded by a first-floor gallery that formed the landing (opposite) to the adjacent staircase (p. 105). The idea of a tall, top-lit tribune at the heart of a house went back to Robert Adam's 1766 Luton Hoo for Lord Bute, a concept taken up by Holland and his partner Capability Brown in Benham Park, Berkshire, which they had designed in 1774. At Carlton House the vestibule was surrounded with portrait busts, by Joseph Nollekens, of the Prince's Whig heroes, Charles James Fox, the Duke of Devonshire, the Duke of Bedford, and Lord Lake. The flashy crimson and gold upholstered benches and curtains are typical of the Empire Style furnishings with which

Walsh Porter, gad-about and decorator-advisor to the Prince, overlaid Holland's more refined work from about 1805 onwards. View by C. Wild.

====================

<u>Staircase Gallery.</u> *The ceiling of this remarkable space at the head of the stairs is an unusual combination of Gothic fan-vaulting and classical details, parallelled only in James Wyatt's*

roughly contemporary entrance hall at Heveningham in Suffolk. An attractive feature of Holland's gallery is the sumptuous blue and gold balustrade in the Louis XVI style of Gabriel. Penetrated by the skylight above, the light well at the centre, and a complex series of arcades on all sides, the upstairs landing at Carlton House must have seemed simultaneously both intimate and open, its essential mystery compounded by the circle of alternating herms and portrait busts. View by C. Wild.

West Ante-Room. By Pyne's day the interiors of Carlton House had been organized in such a way that the rooms for public levees, including the throne room, were ranged along the west front, while the Prince's private audience rooms were along the south front, towards its eastern end. Those attending private audiences would pass directly from the octagonal vestibule or tribune into the ante-room in the south front, but those arriving for public levees would be shown from the threshold of the entrance hall into the west ante-room, seen here in Wild's view. It served as a waiting room for distinguished persons having business to transact with the Prince and for those who had not attained the privilege of entree on state occasions. Noblemen and others of distinction who enjoyed this privilege were shown directly into the circular drawing room in the west wing. The Prince used the west ante-room as a family portrait gallery,

containing, among other pictures, two paintings by Reynolds of the two Dukes of Cumberland, a Hoppner of the Duke of Clarence, and, visible on the far east wall, an oval portrait of George II over the door and the splendid full-length image of the anglophile 'Philippe Égalité', Duc de Chartres and later Duc d'Orléans, a collateral Bourbon (and father of the future King Louis-Philippe) who, incredibly, had voted for the death of Louis XVI. This was painted for the Prince by Reynolds in 1785, eight years before the subject would himself be guillotined. His behaviour towards the martyred French King made him so unpopular in England that the Prince was forced to take the portrait down. View by C. Wild.

OPPOSITE: Ante-Chamber to the Throne Room. Adjacent to the Throne Room on the east was the ante-room, which had served

as a throne room until the Regency. The passions for drapery reminiscent of military tents, which was such a feature of the French Empire style, appears here in the gold-trimmed hangings of light-blue velvet that envelop the north wall and even the mirrors. The same velvet covered the seat furniture. All this richness was doubtless added after 1805 by Walsh Porter, Hopper, Wyatt, or Nash. In this ante-room the Prince hung a collection of family portraits, such as that on the right of Frederick, Duke of York, the Prince's brother-in-law whose Garter-robed image Reynolds painted in 1787–88. View by C. Wild.

Crimson Drawing Room. The west ante-room led directly into the Crimson Drawing Room, which originally functioned as a dining room. The ornamental ceiling, with its deep coves filled with neo-antique stucco work is presumably Holland's of the 1780s, but the room had undergone a complete transformation, beginning in 1808, during which it was enveloped in British-made crimson satin damask, the material used not only for the elaborate curtains but also for covering the sumptuous seat furniture made in c. 1810. Other magnificent additions from this time were the chandeliers, which Pyne rightly regarded as among the finest in Europe, the light-blue velvet carpet, the sub-curtains of white taffeta, the black and gold doors, and the black marble chimney-pieces, supplied by Benjamin Vulliamy in 1808 and now at Windsor Castle. Also surviving in the Royal Collection is the extraordinary French Empire clock of white marble just visible on the chimney-piece in Wild's view. Bought by the Prince in 1809, it is surmounted by a group of bronze figures inspired by those on David's painting entitled The Oath of the Horatii. _Adding richness to richness, the damask-covered walls were hung with major Flemish and Dutch paintings, such as Rubens's_ Landscape with St. George _and_ The Jewish Bride _by the School of Rembrandt._ View by C. Wild.

Circular Room. The Crimson Drawing Room led into the Circular Room that was used at different times as a dining room, music room, and reception hall for formal levees. Holland ringed the room with red porphyry scagliola columns with silver and bronze capitals of the Erectheum Ionic order. The decorative painting, including the sky ceiling, had been executed for Holland by a French painter, either Delabrière or Pernotin, but the extravagant tent-like blue silk drapery and the benches must have been added in c. 1810. View by C. Wild.

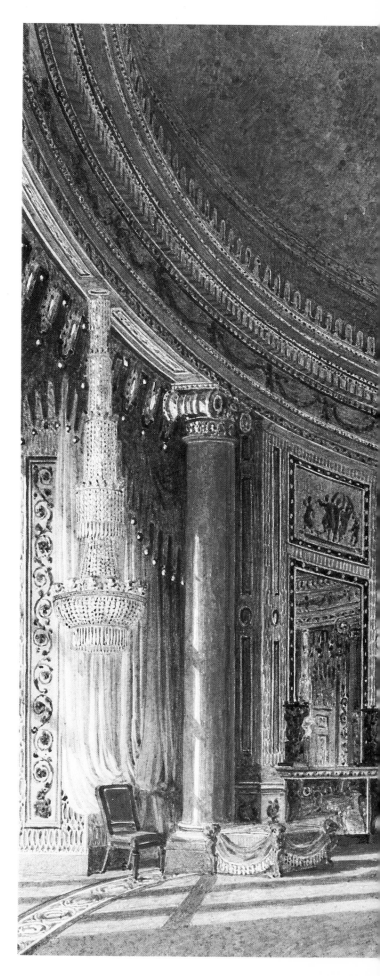

Throne Room. Adjacent to the Circular Room was the Throne Room at the west end of the south front. Originally the Great Drawing Room, it became the Throne Room when the Prince of Wales assumed his Regency in 1811 and needed a larger room than the existing Throne Room next door. The new Throne Room was dominated by an elaborate stuccoed and painted ceiling in the style of Chambers, a work with Raphaelesque grotteschi by Biagio Rebecca that seems to have been painted in 1794. The overdoors, representing the orders of the Garter, the Bath, the St. Patrick, and the St. Andrew, were added by the carver Edward Wyatt when the space became the Throne Room, but the most remarkable addition was the pair of council chairs, almost certainly supplied in 1813 by the firm of Tatham and Co. One of these fantastic objects, which survive at Buckingham Palace, can be seen from the back in the foreground of Wild's watercolour. Made of carved and gilt pine and beechwood, they resemble Roman chariots when viewed from the rear, while on the front they are supported by sphinxes whose wings form the arm rests. Tatham's brother, the architect C.H. Tatham, presumably had a hand in their design, since they depend stylistically on the antique marble seat furniture he had published in his Etchings of Ancient Ornamental Architecture (1799). In 1794–96 Henry Holland had employed C.H. Tatham to collect antique decorative fragments in Rome. Lining the walls of the Throne Room were four pairs of six-light tripod candelabra made of gilt bronze and set on gilt-wood pedestals adorned with garlands and sphinx caryatids, all exquisite pieces of eighteenth-century French craftsmanship that the Prince Regent probably bought in c. 1790 from the marchand-mercier Dominique Daguerre. View by C. Wild.

Ante-Room, looking south. *This view shows us the ante-room to the Prince's blue-velvet suite of private audience rooms beyond (pp.122–123). In deliberate contrast to the splendour of those chambers, its walls received no more elaborate treatment than a coat of bright-blue distemper. However, the room presents a particularly striking example of the imaginative eclecticism practised by the Prince as a collector, both stylistically and iconographically. First, it contains the inevitable family portraits, a kind of painting never distant from his heart, and here we see it in portraits over the doors of five of his far-from-beautiful sisters, the Princesses Augusta, Elizabeth, Mary, Sophia, and Amelia. By contrast, Rubens's magnificent* Young Man with a Hawk *hangs at the centre of the left, or east, wall. Meanwhile, the side-table between the windows must be counted among the Prince's greatest treasures. Acquired in 1816 from the Paris dealer Rocheux, it survives today, a fine Louis XVI piece made of ebony, stamped with Weisweiler's name, and ornamented with gilt-bronze mounts, four* pietra dura *panels, and plaques of red jasper. The bronze statue displayed there represents Louis XV resting on a shield borne by four warriors. Acquired by the Prince in 1813, the statue was made in 1776 by J.-B. Lemyone for a marble monument destined never to be executed. On the left wall stands a large cabinet in the Boulle manner, stamped E. Le Vasseur. It supports a bronze equestrian statue of William III trampling Rebellion underfoot. As a colourful demonstration of the Prince's broad sympathies, this work is balanced on the chimney-piece opposite by a similar statue of William's great enemy, Louis XIV. However, with the chimney-mirror surmounted by an oval portrait of Madame de Pompadour, the whole room becomes a remarkable expression of the Prince's close identification with the style and splendour of the Bourbon court.* View by C. Wild.

Rose Satin Drawing Room, looking north. The walls of this room, at the centre of the garden front, were hung with red satin damask as a sumptuous background for the Prince's collection of Dutch and Flemish paintings. Some of the Dutch works hanging here were among the eighty-six acquired in May 1814 from the collection of Sir Thomas Baring. Much of the Chinoiserie furniture and fittings, including the chimney-piece with its clock and candelabra, had originally been placed in the exquisite Chinese Drawing Room, formed by Henry Holland on the ground floor of the south front in 1789–90. The Prince brought its contents upstairs in c. 1811, at a time when Nash and other architects were remodelling the ground floor. There he exhibited on the tables pieces from his extensive collection of Sèvres and Oriental porcelain. The Sèvres manufactory had enjoyed the special patronage of Louis XV and XVI; thus, the Sèvres assembled by George IV could be seen as an expression of his enthusiasm for the style of the Bourbon monarchy. Moreover, by combining it with Dutch and Flemish paintings, he was consciously echoing French eighteenth-century practice. Indeed, the scenes painted on the porcelain were often taken from pictures by artists such as Teniers the Younger, Wouwermans, and Berchem. View by C. Wild.

Rose Satin Drawing Room, looking south-west. We are reminded once again of the Prince Regent's genius not only as a collector but as a displayer of works of art, for there can be little doubt that his was the guiding hand in the layout of these magnificent rooms of parade. The same red satin damask hung on the walls was used for the curtains, seat furniture, and gold-fringed drapery swags below the cornice, although the artist forgot to include these in this view towards the canted bow-window, with its charming outlook on to the gardens. The carpet, en suite with those in the next three rooms, had gold fleurs-de-lis on a blue ground. This may perhaps be related to the fête given by the Prince to celebrate his Regency in 1811, when he received the exiled French Bourbons in the Blue Velvet suite. The pair of Empire-style candelabra and the pedestals they stood on, one of which can be seen on the left of the door in Wild's watercolour, were acquired in July 1813 from the Thomire workshop in Paris. They survive today at Buckingham Palace. The large painting to the right of the door is The Village Festival _by David Teniers the Younger. On the table in the window stood a magnificent blue Chinese vase with elaborate gilt-bronze mounts probably added by Thomire in 1812._ View by C. Wild.

LEFT ABOVE: <u>Golden Drawing Room.</u> The Lower Vestibule led east into a Gothic library, to which Pyne does not devote a separate illustration, and so into the Golden Drawing Room. This amazing Nash extravaganza was surrounded by fluted, matted-gold columns carrying an imitation rosewood frieze picked out with a gilded anthemion pattern. Large mirrors simply heightened the whole Picturesque drama. The garniture in green Sèvres porcelain on the bookcase to the right of the chimney-piece had been acquired by the Prince in 1813. The central form is a fine vase and cover with dove handles and scenes of hymen and Cupid painted after Boucher. On the chimney-piece stood two brownish-black Sèvres vases with Thomire mounts. View by C. Wild.

LEFT BELOW: <u>Lower Vestibule.</u> The ground-floor rooms along the south front were remodelled between 1807 and 1814 by Wyatt, Nash, and Hopper in an even more flamboyant manner than those above them. Since the rooms were rather low, the hot-house richness of their decoration must have been overpowering. In the Lower Vestibule or Ante-Room of 1813 Nash revealed himself at his most spectacular. Ebonized doors, with arabesque panels in narrow scarlet borders, flanked the green verd-antique scagliola columns crowned by gilded Corinthian columns. The walls were hung with scarlet flock and the scarlet

sofas bordered with black velvet. Dutch and Flemish pictures lined the walls. Between the columns in the centre background of Wild's watercolour we can just see the grand staircase leading up to the principal rooms on the floor above. View by C. Wild.

OVERLEAF: *Golden Drawing Room, alcove.* In July 1822 Sir Thomas Lawrence painted a portrait of the Prince Regent in this sumptuous alcove on the north side of the Golden Drawing Room. The painting shows the royal subject posed behind the round Boulle table seen here, a splendid piece made of rosewood, tortoise shell, and ormolu. Today the portrait is in the Wallace Collection. On the right-hand bookcase stood a garniture of dark-blue Sèvres porcelain. Above both this bookcase and the matching one on the other side of the chimney-piece the Prince had hung paintings by Teniers of villages fêtes. View by C. Wild.

Blue Velvet Room. The principal audience room for ministers of state and ambassadors, the Blue Velvet Room had formed part of the private suite of Princess Caroline after her ill-fated marriage to the Prince in 1795, during which, an irresistible tradition tells us, they spent only one night together. The remodelling of 1811 transformed both it and the Blue Velvet Closet next door into some of the finest state rooms in all of England. The harmony of form and colour of the architectural components and the contents is especially memorable. The walls were hung with dark-blue velvet panels set in peach-coloured borders with gilded frames. This provided the perfect background for such masterpieces as Rembrandt's *Ship Builder and his Wife*, which the Prince had purchased in 1811 for 500 guineas. It is clearly shown in Pyne's view, while the door next to it was one of a set carved and gilded by Edward Wyatt in 1811. Subsequently removed by George IV to Windsor Castle, the doors constitute objects of superlative craftsmanship. On either side of the chimney-piece hung Cuyp's *Passage Boat*, bought by the Prince at the Baring sale in 1814, and Jan Both's *Landscape with St. Philip baptizing the Eunuch*, acquired in 1811. Below the Rembrandt stood a garniture of three blue Sèvres vases on a table flanked by a pair of tall late-eighteenth-century Chinese vases, which, in 1814, the Vulliamy firm had fitted with green marble pedestals and gilt-bronze mounts. Probably also from the 1811 campaign came the ceiling painted as an imitation sky, as well as the paintings of British naval and military triumphs introduced into the coves. The fleurs-de-lis on the carpets in the two preceding rooms had now invaded the curtains and seat-coverings, where they doubtless gave pleasure to the visiting Bourbon exiles. The room contained, in addition, two pairs of superb eight-light candelabra of gilt bronze in the form of female figures holding palm branches, works supplied by Thomire in 1812 and 1813. The writing table is now at Slane Castle, County Meath, Ireland, where it may have been taken, after the death of George IV, by his friend Lord Conyngham. View by C. Wild.

PAGE 124: *Conservatory, looking west. Balancing the Gothic dining room at the east end of the south front was an Ionic dining room at the west end. It led through glass doors into the final* tour de force, *the Gothic conservatory. Created in 1807, this neo-Perpendicular extravaganza of cast-iron and translucent coloured glass was the work of the architect Thomas Hopper. Its fan vault, largely of glass, made a next logical step from King's College Chapel, built in 1446–1515 with walls consisting largely of glass.* View by C. Wild.

PAGE 125: *Conservatory, looking west. In this ravishing watercolour, a fitting conclusion to Pyne's whole enterprise, we look back from the conservatory down the whole length of the lower ground-floor rooms to Nash's Gothic Dining Room at the far west end. The entrance to the Ionic Dining Room is theatrically framed with a proscenium arch of tasselled red drapery. The conservatory provided the setting for the memorable supper party that was the climax of the fête given by the Prince to 2,000 people in June 1811 in celebration of his Regency. The principal supper table, 200 feet long, ran the whole length of the Ionic dining room and Gothic conservatory. Down the middle of the table flowed a stream of water, supplied by a silver fountain in front of the Prince and enlivened with mossy banks, miniature bridges, and goldfish.* View by C. Wild.

Notes and Select Bibliography

Place of publication is London unless otherwise stated.

1. H.M. Colvin, ed., *History of the King's Works*, V (1976), p. 131.
2. J. Pote, *History and Antiquities of Windsor Castle* (Eton, 1749), p. 423.
3. D. Lysons, *Environs of London*, III (1795), p. 185.
4. Colvin, *op. cit.*, p. 73.
5. J. Book, *King George III* (1972), p. 282.
6. E.J. Climenson, ed., *Passages from the Diaries of Mrs. Philip Lybbe Powys…
   1756–1808* (1809), p. 116.
7. O. Hedley, *Queen Charlotte* (1975), p. 180.
8. Horace Walpole to the Countess of Upper Ossory, 17 September 1785.
9. H. Wyndham, ed., *Correspondence of Sarah Spencer, Lady Lyttelton*
   (1912), pp. 103–104.
10. Robinson to Carlisle, 23 December 1734, *Historical Manuscripts
    Commission Report*, 42, Carlisle MSS, pp. 143–144.

Beattie, J.M. *The English Court in the Reign of George I*. Cambridge, 1967.
Bellaigue, G. de. 'The Furnishings of the Chinese Drawing Room, Carlton
        House', *Burlington Magazine*, September 1967, pp. 518–528.
Brook, J. *King George III*. 1972.
*Collection of Ordinances and Regulations for the Government of the Royal
        Household made in reigns from King Edward III to King William and
        Queen Mary*. Society of Antiquaries, 1790.
Colvin, H.M. *Biographical Dictionary of British Architects, 1660–1840*. 1978.
———, ed. *History of the King's Works* (especially vol. V, *1660–1782*, 1976, and vol.
        VI, *1782–1851)*. 1973.
Cornforth, J. *Pyne's Royal Residences* (Folio Miniatures). 1976.
Croft-Murray, E. *Decorative Painting in England, 1537–1837*, 2 vols. 1962–70.
Downes, K. *English Baroque Architecture*. 1966.
Fowler, J., and J. Cornforth. *English Decoration in the 18th Century*. 1966.
Fulford, R. *George the Fourth*. 1935.
Green, D.B. *Grinling Gibbons*. 1964.
Harris, J. *Sir William Chambers*. 1970.
———, et al. *Buckingham Palace*. 1968.
Hedley, O. *Queen Charlotte*. 1975.
Hibbert, C. *The Court at Windsor, a Domestic History*. 1964.
Hussey, C. 'Kensington Palace', *Country Life*, LVI, 1924, pp. 838–887, 884–894,
        952–958; LVII, 1925, pp. 56-63; LXIV, 1928, pp. 296–302.
———. 'Windsor Castle', *Country Life*, LXVIII, 1930, pp. 708–716, 751–754,
        776–782, 785–788, 802–808, 813–815.
———, and A.I. Dasent. 'St James's Palace', *Country Life*, LIII, 1923, pp. 82–88,
        142–155.
Laking, G.F. *The Furniture of Windsor Castle*. 1905.

Law, E. *History of Hampton Court*, 3 vols. 1885–91.

Levey, M. *Later Italian Pictures in the Royal Collection*. 1964.

Linstrum, D. *Sir Jeffry Wyatville*. 1972.

Mackworth-Young, R. *Windsor Castle*. 1982.

Millar, O. *Tudor, Stuart and Early Georgian Pictures in the Royal Collection*, 2 vols. 1963.

———. *Later Georgian Pictures in the Royal Collection*, 2 vols. 1969.

Morshead, O. *Windsor Castle*. 1951.

Murray-Baillie, H. 'Etiquette and the Planning of the State Apartments in Baroque Palaces', *Archaeologia*, CI, 1967.

Myers, A.R. *Household of Edward IV*. Manchester, 1959.

Oppé, A.P. *English Drawings, Stuart and Georgian Periods, in the Collection of H.M. the King at Windsor Castle*. 1950.

Pote, J. *History and Antiquities of Windsor Castle*. Eton, 1749.

Queen's Gallery, Buckingham Palace, Exhibition Catalogues:
  George IV and the Arts of France. 1966.
  George III – Collector and Patron. 1974–75.
  Sèvres – Porcelain from the Royal Collection. 1979–80.

Roberts, J. 'Henry Emlyn's Restoration of St George's Chapel', *Report of the Society of the Friends of St George's*, V, no. 8, 1876–77, pp. 331–338.

Robinson, J.M. *The Wyatts, an Architectural Dynasty*. Oxford, 1979.

———. *Royal Residences*. London and Sydney, 1982.

St. John Hope, W.H. *Windsor Castle, an Architectural History*, 2 vols. 1913.

Shearman, J. *Earlier Italian Pictures in the Royal Collection*. Cambridge, 1983.

Smith, H. Clifford. *Buckingham Palace*. 1931.

Stroud, D. *Henry Holland*. 1966.

Summerson, Sir J. *Architecture in Britain, 1530–1830*. Harmondsworth, 1953 (5th ed. 1969).

Survey of London, XX, 1940 (for Carlton House).

Watson, F. 'Holland and Daguerre: French undercurrents in English Neo-Classic Furniture Design', *Apollo*, October 1972, pp. 282–287.

Webb, M.I. *Michael Rysbrack, Sculptor*. 1954.

White, C. *The Dutch Pictures in the Collection of Her Majesty the Queen*. Cambridge, 1982.

Wren Society Publications, 20 vols. (especially VII, *Royal Palaces of Winchester, Whitehall, Kensington and St James's*). 1924–43.